HARRY

HARRY

A BIOGRAPHY

MARCIA MOODY

Michael O'Mara Books Limited

First published in Great Britain in 2014 by
Michael O'Mara Books Limited
9 Lion Yard
Tremadoc Road
London SW4 7NQ

A CIP catalogue record for this book is available from the British Library.

Papers used by Michael O'Mara Books Limited are natural, recyclable products
made from wood grown in sustainable forests. The manufacturing processes
conform to the environmental regulations of the country of origin.

ISBN: 978-1-78243-037-7 in hardback print format
ISBN: 978-1-78243-172-5 in paperback print format
ISBN: 978-1-78243-042-1 in ebook format

1 2 3 4 5 6 7 8 9 10

www.mombooks.com

Designed and typeset by Billy Waqar

Printed and bound by CPI Group (UK) Ltd, Croydon CR0 4YY

Contents

CONTENTS

Introduction

For the past twenty-nine years, Prince Harry has been one of the most famous people in the country, and although at times controversial, he has attracted both criticism and praise. He has been to war, trekked in the Arctic and motorbiked across Africa. He has set up his own charities championing the wounded and the forgotten, represented his grandmother the Queen overseas, and won a humanitarian award. He also happens to have a liking for plunging into swimming pools fully clothed, jumping off things, climbing up things, and generally making sure he is in the middle of whatever is going on. And if there's nothing much going on, then he will make sure something is done about that. He grabs life with both hands and rides it at 100 miles an hour – sometimes perilously close to the edge.

He sees himself as three different figures – the soldier, the man and the prince – equally at home on the battlefield or the polo field, in England's green and pleasant land, or in the wilds of Africa. However, he has always felt less comfortable in his royal role, sometimes struggling with the constant attention it brings. His mother, Diana Princess of Wales, inspired such love and devotion from not just the people of the UK, but all around the world, that they felt as though they actually knew her. It was different from what previous supporters of the royal family had felt – with their strong sense of pride, admiration and respect – this was emotional. People were as fiercely protective, fond and invested in Diana as if she was family or a dear friend. In the same way, interest in her two sons was always going to be high. When William and Harry were born in the wake of what was billed as a fairy-tale wedding, it was a cause for countrywide celebration. People were also therefore fascinated to watch her boys grow up.

Almost from the beginning of the Prince and Princess of Wales's marriage, public opinion about the couple was divided and people chose sides. If they liked Diana they may not have had a lot of fondness or sympathy for Charles, and vice versa. Prince Harry loves his father and loved his mother very much, and he has also grown to love his stepmother Camilla, Duchess of Cornwall. So this book is written with that in mind, endeavouring to present a balanced portrait of each individual. All three are human beings with flaws and idiosyncrasies and, as with all of us, they have made mistakes over the years. None of them are perfect, but none of them are bad people.

William will one day be King, and so the main spotlight has always shone more squarely on him. However, Harry has never been one to stay in the shadows, and as he approaches his thirtieth birthday it seems a good time to look at the man behind the very famous name. The bold, colourful and interesting character who is known and loved around the world is one part of him, but his subtleties and nuances are perhaps less well known. As a very little boy, Harry was a sensitive, shy thumb-sucker who was prone to carsickness, while older brother William was the loud, outgoing, rough-and-tumble one. It wasn't long before they switched roles, and Harry became the hot-headed, outspoken sibling, while William has become more measured and diplomatic. There are still times now when the quieter, more vulnerable side of Harry shines through, and those moments certainly help to build a clearer picture of the man he has become.

CHAPTER ONE

The Family

'It's a boy!' Three words excitedly shouted out by a television crewman, announced to the world the birth of the new royal baby. With that, the crowds outside the hospital cheered, and a motorist not looking where he was going drove into the side of an ambulance. It was not the most decorous of introductions for the new third in line to the throne, but it signified the excitement a new generation of royals was beginning to generate in the British public.

In 1984 Britain was still riding a wave of royal euphoria that had started four years earlier, when the Prince of Wales began his courtship of blushing kindergarten teacher Lady Diana Spencer, and a reticent star was born. The British public were immediately endeared to the shy and beautiful nineteen-year-old, and after just six months her engagement to the first in line to the throne was announced. After marrying in 1981, Charles and Diana welcomed their first son, Prince William, the following year, and their second son two years later at 4.20 p.m.

on Saturday 15 September 1984. Although the newborn's given name was Prince Henry Charles Albert David, it was announced that he would always be known as Harry. Diana later said, 'Royal first-borns may get all the glory, but second-borns enjoy more freedom. Only when Harry is a lot older will he realize how lucky he is not to have been the eldest.'

On the morning of 15 September, the heavily pregnant – but still a week away from her due date – Princess Diana had stirred early in Windsor Castle, where she and Prince Charles were staying. Her second son may have been a week early, but he was ready. Outside, it was a misty early-autumn morning as Charles and Diana, accompanied by their bodyguard, left the castle at 6.30 a.m., drove the thirty minutes into London and checked into St Mary's Hospital, Paddington. It was a familiar drill, as they were once again based in the private Lindo Wing, where Diana had given birth to William, making their older son the first heir to the throne to be born in hospital. Charles had been born in the Belgian Suite of Buckingham Palace, while before him all other royals had also been born at home. However, Diana showed signs of things to come when she pushed to modernize the tradition, and insisted on giving birth in a hospital. This time, with Harry, it was no different, and once more the attending gynaecologist was Mr George Pinker, who was at the time the Queen's surgeon-gynaecologist and a senior consultant at St Mary's.

Charles and Diana arrived at the Lindo Wing at 7.30 a.m., and outside the hospital as the day progressed 300 press and onlookers jostled behind a double row of police barriers. Inside, however, all was surprisingly calm. Diana read a book for the first six hours of labour, and took no drugs, as Charles, dressed in a hospital gown, dozed in a chair next to her. At times he fed her ice cubes as a nurse administered lip balm, and then when the grey sky darkened, their second son finally made his entrance at 4.20 p.m. – blue-eyed, russet-haired and weighing 6lb 14oz. The room was jubilant, and one hospital worker revealed that when he visited the suite everyone was laughing.

While two forty-one-gun salutes cracked the air – one in Hyde Park and the second simultaneously from the Tower of London – a town cryer in plumed hat called out 'Her Royal Highness the Princess Diana has issued forth a second son!' However, it turned out that this particular individual had no official role, and had been hired by a Japanese television company.

News of Harry's birth was posted on the gates of Balmoral where the Queen and Duke of Edinburgh were staying, and the Queen went to church led by pipers. At Heathrow Airport, after the announcement of the birth was made in several languages, sticks of rock and postcards were given out to passengers. Two hours later a beaming Charles emerged to shake hands with the crowds and received a baby's dummy from one well-wisher, telling another, 'My wife is very well. The delivery couldn't have been better. It was much quicker this time.' While inside the princess cradled her tiny newborn.

The next day, as people massed six-deep outside the hospital, Charles pulled up with a two-year-old Prince William, who was dressed in a white shirt and red shorts to meet his new baby brother. The young William was something of a handful and Diana's brother Charles Spencer had noted on Harry's birth, 'It will be lovely for William to have a companion and a playmate ... someone to fight with.' After waving to the crowds, the exuberant William disappeared inside with his father and *People* magazine reported that he belted down the corridor to his mother's room, who, on hearing him approach, opened the door and said gently, 'Wills, darling, come here.'

Two hours later, as nurses watched from the windows and the excited crowds waved union flags and cheered hip hip hooray, Diana emerged in a scarlet puff-sleeved coat and with a voluminous blow dry, cradling her newborn son in her arms. With Charles by her side, she paused on the top step as the flashbulbs exploded, and then slipped into the car with her husband, as they headed off to Kensington Palace. Years later, when William and his wife the Duchess of Cambridge left the very same hospital with their newborn Prince George, it was a sign of how times had changed that George was strapped into a baby-seat before William drove them home. In 1984, as was the practice with all parents of the time, Diana simply sat in the car with baby Harry still in her arms as they drove to Kensington Palace.

As Diana set about settling Harry in, Charles honoured a prior commitment by playing in a local polo match. It had been scheduled for some time and Charles didn't want to let anyone down, but unfortunately Diana felt abandoned – and it wasn't the first time she had felt that way. When she was a month away from her due date with Harry, she attended the funeral of her favourite uncle, Lord Fermoy, who after threatening suicide on a previous occasion, had shot himself. As it was customary for royals to only attend the funerals of their own relatives, Diana drove down from Balmoral without her husband. Dressed in a black silk maternity dress, she cut a lonely figure.

*

The first flush of romance between Charles and Diana saw them engaged after just six months, however it wasn't long before problems started to arise between them. The first year of married life for Charles and Diana – which for the most part Diana spent pregnant with William – was at times happy. However, her fears that there was more than just friendship between her husband and his former girlfriend Camilla Parker Bowles had an impact on her psychological well-being, and along with struggling to cope with life behind palace walls, contributed to her suffering from bulimia. So when Harry was born, although the marriage was only three years old, it was already in deep trouble.

Gyles Brandreth revealed in his book *Charles and Camilla* that Diana's close friend Rosa Monckton told him, 'The root of all her problems was her early life. It was so damaged. She talked a lot about that. She talked particularly about the feeling of being abandoned – abandoned by her mother when she was a little girl, abandoned by her father when he married Raine.'

Diana was from an aristocratic background – the third daughter of Earl Spencer and Frances Ruth Roche, whose family had been linked to royalty for three centuries. Both of Diana's grandmothers – Cynthia, Countess Spencer, and Ruth, Lady Fermoy – had been the Queen Mother's ladies-in-waiting, and her maternal grandfather was an equerry to King George VI (the Queen's father), and, later, the Queen. Therefore, when Diana's parents married in Westminster Abbey, the Queen and Duke of Edinburgh, the Queen Mother and Princess Margaret were guests, while the Queen is godmother to Diana's brother Charles, and the Queen Mother was godmother to her sister Sarah. As a child, Diana and her siblings would play with Prince Andrew, who would visit the Spencer family home, Park House, an impressive mansion nestled on a sprawling estate not far from Sandringham, the Queen's Norfolk home.

After Diana's elder sisters Sarah and Jane were born, the Spencers welcomed a son, however their happiness was short-lived as he died ten hours later, leaving both parents distraught. Diana was conceived the same year, and always felt that her parents had wanted her to be a boy, to replace the son who had passed away, and she felt unwanted. She later told Andrew Morton for his book *Diana: Her True Story*, 'The child who died before me was a son and both [parents] were crazy to have a son and heir and there comes a third daughter. What a bore, we're going to have to try again.' Adding, 'At the age of fourteen I just remember thinking I wasn't very good at anything, that I was hopeless ...'

Her parents went on to have another son, Charles, who was born three years after Diana, but their parents' marriage was in trouble and soon afterwards Frances fell in love with another man, Peter Shand Kydd, and left the marital home.

It had been known that the Spencers had been in an unhappy marriage for some time, and Diana's childhood was marked with lots of memories of her mother crying and her younger brother crying. 'It was a very unhappy childhood,' Diana revealed.

When Diana was fourteen, her father married Raine, Countess of Dartmouth, daughter of the romance novelist Dame Barbara Cartland. Diana and her siblings disliked Raine, who took charge of their family home. However, when their father collapsed with a cerebral haemorrhage and was in a coma for four months, developing a life-threatening abscess on his lung, Raine found a new drug in Germany that saved his life, and the children later acknowledged this. Diana continued to feel the effects of her parents' break-up, combatting her feelings of loneliness by filling her bed with stuffed animals. However, when she went away to boarding school she was only allowed to take one animal with her, so she chose a green hippo, painting its eyes with luminous paint so in the dark it would appear to be looking at her.

As a teenager she was shy and introverted – she didn't like clubbing, drinking or smoking – but she was a happier teen than she had been as a child. She made close girlfriends and moved into a flat in Earls Court, West London, with three of them, one of whom was Carolyn Pride who later became Harry's godmother. Diana got a job at Young England Kindergarten, and in her spare time she liked watching TV, listening to pop music and reading fashion magazines and the novels of her step-grandmother, Barbara Cartland. She was still immature, and she and her friends would make prank calls, or throw flour and eggs over the cars of those they felt had slighted them. She dated assorted eligible young men but on her wedding day she was a virgin bride – as she told Andrew Morton, 'I knew I had to keep myself tidy for what lay ahead.'

Because of the links between her family and the royal family, she had known Charles since she was born but the twelve-year age difference meant they had not been playmates. Her childhood friends were his younger brothers Prince Andrew and Prince Edward, while Charles had originally dated Diana's older sister Sarah, and they went skiing together to the Swiss resort Klosters. As a teenager, Diana was attracted to Charles but believed herself to be podgy and unsophisticated, however she caught his eye at a friend's barbecue in the late summer of 1980. She had just turned nineteen and Charles later said he was drawn to her because of her wonderful 'girlish bounce'.

Charles had had a traditional royal upbringing, in the early years of his life spending more time with beloved nannies than with his parents. At the time of his birth, his mother was twenty-two-year-old Princess Elizabeth and her father the King had terminal cancer. There was already a lot of pressure on her young shoulders, as she was becoming more involved with royal life, and was undertaking those of King George's engagements that he couldn't manage. It meant that she would see the infant Charles for thirty minutes in the morning after he was bathed and fed, and an hour and a half in the evening when she played with him, bathed him and put him to bed. Charles's father Prince Philip was serving in the navy and was stationed in Malta at the time, which meant he wasn't home as much as he would have liked.

When his grandfather King George VI died in 1952, Charles was three and his baby sister Princess Anne was a year old. Their mother became Queen at the age of twenty-five and as a woman in a man's world of military, politics and overseas heads of state, she felt like she had a lot to prove. The monarchy had been rocked by the abdication of her uncle just one generation before, and she felt the pressure of maintaining a stable institution, recognizing the importance of devoting herself to her people, and throwing herself into her duties. Charles was a sensitive and not very confident boy and his parents' absence affected him more than they realized – as well as the day-to-day routine of his life, they would often leave him and his sister in the care of their grandparents and nannies to embark on the overseas royal tours that their position required. Although he had been joined by younger sister Anne when he was two, he led a fairly isolated existence behind palace walls as he was home-schooled until the age of eight.

As he grew into a young boy, and then a teenager, Charles forged a very close relationship with his grandmother the Queen Mother, as well as his nanny Mabel Anderson, and would often turn to them for advice instead of his parents. He loved and respected his mother and father, and appreciated them more and more as he grew older, but the lines of communication were more open with his grandmother and nanny at that time. When he went away to boarding school at Gordonstoun, he pined for home. He was prone to sinus problems and tonsillitis, which caused ragged breathing at night and led to friction with the other boys in his dorm who couldn't sleep. In his late teens and early twenties he became a more confident young adult, and after a few dalliances, he first met the vivacious Camilla Shand at a polo match in the summer of 1971. He was twenty-three and she was twenty-four, and had been in a previous relationship with Andrew Parker Bowles, a captain in the Household Cavalry. However, the attraction between Charles and Camilla was instant and strong, and they began a relationship. Camilla was a debutante and her family had ties to the royal family, as her great-grandmother Alice Keppel had been the mistress of King Edward VII. The young lovebirds also shared a slightly off-beat sense of humour and had a love of the big outdoors and country pursuits. Charles and Camilla developed strong feelings for each other, however they were both still young, and Charles had a lifetime of duty ahead of him. He wasn't ready to settle down yet and was also about to embark on his military career in the navy, which would see him away at sea for prolonged periods. After a year together they split up and Charles moved forwards with his naval career.

Camilla went back to Andrew Parker Bowles and they became engaged the following year. Charles was on his ship in the Caribbean and on hearing the news he wrote to his great-uncle and mentor Lord Mountbatten of the announcement, 'I suppose the feeling of emptiness will pass eventually.'

Decades later, when his sons William and Harry split with their first serious girlfriends Kate Middleton and Chelsy Davy, they both – perhaps mindful of their father's decision to let Camilla go when he was a young man – got back together with them to give it another go. They simply didn't want to let go of the woman they loved – even if they did feel too young for a big commitment.

Charles and Camilla stayed in touch, and throughout the remainder of the seventies they would write to each other and speak on the phone – he would visit her at home and they would spend hours talking. When Lord Mountbatten was killed by an IRA bomb in 1979, Charles turned to Camilla for comfort. Despite Charles's feelings for Camilla, he was all too aware of the events surrounding the relationship between his great-uncle Edward VIII and Wallis Simpson – just forty years earlier Edward's refusal to give up his relationship with the divorcee meant he abdicated the throne.

Charles was, however, ready to start a family, and at the age of thirty-one was under a certain amount of pressure to settle down, and this is when he crossed paths with Diana again. She was asked to join a weekend away by their mutual friend Philip de Pass, and they found themselves sitting on a hay bale together at a barbecue where they chatted. She recounted in *Diana: Her True Story* that she told him, 'You looked so sad when you walked up the aisle at Lord Mountbatten's funeral. It was the most tragic thing I've ever seen. My heart bled for you when I watched. I thought it's wrong, you're lonely – you should be with someone to look after you.'

Charles was moved by her kindness and warmth, and asked her out. Their first date was a classical music concert at the Royal Albert Hall followed by a cold supper at Buckingham

Palace. Although it was 1980, it was still traditional in such circumstances for Diana to be accompanied by a chaperone, and the couple were joined by her grandmother Ruth Fermoy. Charles then invited Diana to Balmoral for the annual Braemar Games on the first Saturday in September, where Diana joined in with many of the outdoor activities.

It was in Scotland that the press found out about Charles and Diana's fledgling relationship, and from that point on Diana became a public figure. Photographers camped outside her flat, reporters knocked on her door and called her on the phone, while the more unscrupulous members of the press went through her rubbish bins. On one occasion Diana ditched her car and got on to a bus in order to shake off those who were following her, and on another, using bed sheets, she lowered luggage out of the back window of her flat; it became common practice for her to switch cars with family members and friends.

Diana's mother Frances was alarmed by the nature of the sudden interest in her daughter and wrote a letter to *The Times*, 'In recent weeks many articles have been labelled exclusive quotes, when the plain truth is my daughter has not spoken the words attributed to her. Fanciful speculation if it is in good taste is one thing, but this can be embarrassing. Lies are quite another matter and by their very nature, hurtful and inexcusable ... May I ask the editors of Fleet Street, whether in the execution of their jobs, they consider it necessary or fair to harass my daughter from dawn until well after dusk?'

It was against this backdrop that the Duke of Edinburgh wrote to his son Charles, suggesting that he needed to make his mind up about whether he was serious about Diana, because it wasn't fair on her and might ruin her reputation if, for Charles, this was merely a casual relationship. Within just a few months the people of Great Britain had fallen in love with the pretty nineteen-year-old, but had Prince Charles?

Charles took his father's words to heart. After some thought, he proposed in early February 1981, and their engagement was announced on 24 February. Engagement pictures showed the prince and his fiancée on the steps of Buckingham Palace, with Diana in a royal-blue skirt suit with pussycat bow blouse, and the sapphire and diamond ring on her wedding finger, which was to become perhaps the most famous ring in the world. That evening, Diana moved from her girl's flat in Earls Court into an apartment in Clarence House, which was the Queen Mother's home. Charles was living at Buckingham Palace at the time, so it would not have been appropriate for her to move in with him under the same roof before the wedding. Charles wasn't at Clarence House to greet her when she arrived, but there was a handwritten note from Camilla reading, 'Such exciting news about the engagement. Do let's have lunch when the Prince of Wales goes to Australia and New Zealand. He's going to be away for three weeks. I'd love to see the ring. Lots of love, Camilla.'

Diana always said she knew there was 'someone else on the scene' from the very early days of her and Charles's relationship. Camilla had been his girlfriend but she was also now his best friend, so while she might have been wearing the 'best friend' hat when she wrote the letter, the fact remained that Camilla had also been more than that to the prince. Perhaps the roles were clearly defined in the heads of Charles and Camilla, but they were certainly not for Diana. Additionally, she was shocked and overwhelmed in her new world. Centuries of protocol and formality ran through the generations of the royal family, but there was no cause to believe that Diana would need help to be guided through – she was, after all, from the aristocracy herself. However, the world outside royal walls had changed immeasurably since the then Princess Elizabeth had married Lieutenant Philip Mountbatten in 1952. The world had modernized, but the royal family had not, and Diana was the first person to marry an heir to the throne post-1960s.

Additionally, Charles was already heavily involved in royal duty. Nearly every day he was in a different part of the country and almost immediately after Diana moved in, he had to leave for five weeks on an overseas tour. Charles had been raised to do his duty, as countless generations of royals had before him, and had a practical approach to relationships, whereas Diana's teenage years had been fuelled by a diet of romantic novels and she had never had a 'proper' boyfriend, so had a child-like view of love and romance. Unbeknownst to anyone else, Diana started suffering from bulimia, and expressed to those close to her concerns about whether she was making the right decision in getting married, but her sisters reminded her that it was a little late, as her face was 'already on the tea towels'.

Charles was shocked that Diana had gone from glowing girlfriend to troubled princess-in-waiting, and didn't understand her emotional nature. He was used to measured communication and if he couldn't comprehend her mood he would often walk away in frustration, which just made Diana worse. They were both people who needed comfort, but even in the early stages of their relationship they didn't get it from each other. However, at that point they were still getting to know each other and hoped that things would improve.

Their wedding was a cause for countrywide celebration, and three months afterwards, Diana was pregnant. At that time the year before, she had been a single girl living with her girlfriends. Things had moved very fast. She had gone from nursery teacher to princess, single girl to wife, and chaste teenager to expectant mother in less than a year. And she was still just twenty years old and followed constantly by the photographers. The press office at Buckingham Palace was unused to dealing with the hysteria and fervour that accompanied Diana's intoxicating popularity – they thought it would die down after the wedding, but it just increased. While Diana was pregnant with William, the Queen invited all newspaper editors to Buckingham Palace, where her press secretary appealed to them to stop harassing her daughter-in-law and allow her private life to be private.

Diana suffered morning sickness and stress when she was pregnant with William, was sick throughout the labour and suffered post-natal depression afterwards. However, she and Charles both adored parenthood and doted on their baby son. Diana discovered she was pregnant again in January 1984, when William was seven months old. She later called the years in between her sons' births as 'total darkness' but she added that she and Charles were 'very very close to each other' in the run up to Harry's birth. The second pregnancy was tough too and she again suffered with morning sickness, but she performed more public engagements and was more sociable. 'Then suddenly as Harry was born it just went bang, our marriage, the whole thing went down the drain', she later told Andrew Morton. This is the family life into which Harry was born. He and his brother were adored by both parents, while their own personal lives were in tumult.

CHAPTER TWO

Flak and shrapnel of thundercracks

One-day-old Harry was wrapped in a soft white blanket and taken back to his parents' home in Kensington Palace. The residence in West London had always been a favourite of the royal family, and Charles and Diana had selected it as their first marital home, moving in immediately after their wedding, three years earlier. In 1689 Kensington Palace, originally a Jacobean mansion, had been bought by King William III from the Earl of Nottingham because the king had asthma and wanted to move from the palace in Whitehall on the banks of the Thames, to somewhere where the air was clean and fresh. Kensington Palace was certainly that, set in beautifully landscaped gardens that have further bloomed in size and content over the years. In 1762, George III had turned the palace into apartments for the royal family and grace-and-favour apartments for the royal household – gifts from the Queen that have no or nominal rent. Princess Victoria was just eighteen when she woke in her bedroom in

Kensington Palace to discover she was Queen. When Harry and William were growing up, their neighbours included Princess Margaret and Diana's sister Lady Jane Fellowes, who had also married into royal life as her husband was the private secretary to the Queen. The Fellowes also lived at Kensington Palace with their two (later three) children – Harry and William's cousins.

Charles and Diana occupied apartments 8 and 9, where there were three reception rooms, a dining room, three bedrooms and, on the top floor, a whole nursery suite. It was not a vast and cavernous home, but had – for a palace – modest-sized rooms, and a fresh, light colour scheme. Although each room featured antique tables, paintings, tapestries and marble fireplaces, they blended with the contemporary decor, which was the work of Dudley Poplak, the South African designer that Diana's mother had recommended. The drawing room, where the couple met their guests, was painted lemon yellow and furnished with sofas and armchairs in sherbet shades of orange, yellow and green. It also contained a Steinway grand piano, which Diana could play. The sitting room had a lighter watercolour palette, with duck-egg blue patterned wallpaper and smoky pink sofas. The nursery was nestled on the top floor under the eaves and, according to royal tradition, this was where the young Harry and William would spend most of their time in the first few years of their lives.

The nursery suite was made up of bedrooms for the boys, nannies and protection officers, bathrooms, a playroom, kitchen and dining room. It was painted in yellow and white, with a strawberry print carpet, and was decorated by luxury children's design company Dragons of Walton Street with animal stencils. The playroom was filled with stuffed animals and painted wooden toys, including a pair of rocking horses. Diana had been shopping in Harrods for Harry, but one of his favourite playthings became a Snoopy soft toy that belonged to his mother.

Charles and Diana were full-time working members of the royal family and Diana was back performing public engagements within two months of Harry being born, so the boys had two nannies – one full time and one deputy. The main nanny, Barbara Barnes, had been employed when William was born, and she was old-fashioned and strict. Both boys loved her and called her Baba. All went well to begin with. Under Diana's instruction – and in a break from royal tradition – the nannies did not wear a uniform, and they were referred to by their first names. Barbara's deputy, Olga Powell, started when William was six months old and stayed as deputy through three full-time nannies, until the boys were old enough not to need a nanny anymore, meaning she was one of the most dependable and formative presences throughout the young boys' lives.

It was a traditional royal set-up, and it was how Charles had been raised. Although he had felt a distance between himself and his parents when he was growing up, Charles believed that as long as he was around more for his sons, then the presence of nannies was as it should be. Diana, however, grew to be unhappy with the situation. She had felt neglected as a child and was determined that her children wouldn't feel the same way, so wanted to be more involved with the boys than Barbara was used to with her previous clients.

It was customary for palace staff to meet new additions to the family in a line-up but once more Diana broke with tradition and invited the two cooks, her dressers, the housekeeper and the butler to have drinks with her in the sitting room. Harry settled in and both parents doted on their young sons. Diana commented that Charles loved 'nursery life' and would read his sons stories. He used to make them laugh by pulling silly faces and putting on voices. Harry was a good baby – he never cried and was always smiling. However, as a toddler, William was used to being the centre of attention and was something of a handful. Harry's christening took place on 21 December 1984 in St George's Chapel, Windsor, and William was frustrated that he wasn't allowed to hold his brother. Harry was wearing a 143-year-old christening gown, and no one trusted the toddler prince to be around it. Photographer Lord Snowdon came up with the idea of William playing with an antique bird cage to keep him occupied long enough to get the group shots with the Queen and Duke of Edinburgh, the Queen Mother, Charles, Diana and Harry's godparents. Lord Snowdon's assistant later said of William, 'Every time he did something naughty they all roared with laughter. No one admonished him and he was being a thorough pest.'

Heirs to the throne are always christened in the Music Room at Buckingham Palace, but since this was not to be Harry's fate, his christening was at the Queen's beloved Windsor Castle, which is where Diana had woken on the day she gave birth to him. It had been built by William the Conqueror in the eleventh century, and was home and final resting place to many of Harry's ancestor's. Henry VIII was buried there along with the wife he requested to be lain next to, Jane Seymour; and Elizabeth I spent most of her time living in Windsor Castle. It was also the principal residence for Queen Victoria and Prince Albert; where the Queen Mother was laid to rest; and where Charles and Camilla's eventual marriage was blessed.

Harry's christening was full of royal tradition. He was baptised with holy water from the Jordan River, and the service was conducted by the Archbishop of Canterbury, Dr Robert Runcie. The three-month-old prince also wore the flowing white gown of Honiton lace lined with white satin that had been made for Queen Victoria's daughter, and in which every royal baby since had been christened. Like his older brother, Harry had six godparents who were all in attendance: Lady Armstrong-Jones, the daughter of Princess Margaret and Lord Snowdon; painter Bryan Organ who was one of Charles's friends; soldier, stockbroker and sportsman Gerald Ward – another of Charles's friends; Prince Andrew, the Duke of York; Diana's old flatmate Carolyn Bartholomew (née Pride); and Lady Cece Vestey, a friend of the Queen.

In a break from tradition, however, the christening was filmed and televised along with the Queen's annual Christmas message a few days later. William was shown running round the Archbishop of Canterbury's legs in pursuit of his cousin Zara Philips, as her older brother Peter tried to grab him, before Charles scooped him up in a hug. Charles's friend, Poet Laureate Ted Hughes, wrote a poem to commemorate the event called 'Rain Charm for the Duchy: A Blessed, Devout Drench for the Christening of His Royal Highness Prince Harry'. It spoke of an almighty rainstorm nourishing the land after a drought. Many commented there didn't seem an obvious connection between the content and the event it was to commemorate, but it was noted that there was an historic link between the fertility of royalty and the health of the land. In the epic description of nature unleashed, there were also references to the royal and military themes that would run through Harry's life, with mention of a sky heaped up with 'mayoral pomp', and thunder: a 'brass band accompaniment', while the 'flak and shrapnel of thundercracks hit the wall and roofs'. Harry didn't just receive his own poem to mark his christening – Barry Manilow sent him a valuable five-inch baby grand piano.

In the Queen's Christmas message that year she paid tribute to her newest grandchild, and it was clear she had been affected by his birth, saying: 'The happy arrival of our fourth grandchild gave great cause for family celebrations. But for parents and grandparents, a birth is also a time for reflection on what the future holds for the baby and how they can best ensure its safety and happiness. To do that, I believe we must be prepared to learn as much from them as they do from us. We could use some of that sturdy confidence and devastating honesty with which children rescue us from self-doubts and self-delusions. We could borrow that unstinting trust of the child in its parents for our dealings with each other.'

*

Harry settled into nursery life at Kensington Palace, while William got used to sharing his parents' attention with his new baby brother. They had a large extended family and spent time with their grandparents, aunts, uncles and cousins on both sides. They called the Queen Mother 'Gran Gran', the Queen was 'Granny', Prince Philip 'Grandpa' and Diana's mother 'Granny Frances'. They called their parents 'Papa' and 'Mummy'.

William was heir to the throne, while Harry was 'the spare', which meant that William often received the lion's-share of attention from some senior members of the family, as well as some of the staff. The Queen Mother used to put a seat next to her and call for William to sit on it, and he also used to go to Clarence House, without Harry, to see her.

Helping to prepare her great-grandson for what lay ahead was one thing, but according to a former palace employee, the boys' first nanny also treated the two boys differently. Inspector

Ken Wharfe was William and Harry's personal protection officer from 1986 to 1988 and then Diana's until 1993. He therefore saw Harry grow from a two-year-old toddler into a nine-year-old boy, and remembers: 'Barbara favoured William far more than Harry, which didn't appeal to Diana. I remember a few trips down to Highgrove with Barbara when Harry was very small, and he would be ignored almost to the point where it didn't really matter what happened to him. He was quite prone to carsickness and we used to have to stop several times on the M4 for him to – poor bloke – throw up on the hard shoulder. I used to say, "Maybe he should see someone about this", and she would say, "Oh, he's all right. He's fine."'

Charles and Diana, however, were very aware of Harry not feeling like just 'the spare' and they treated both of their sons equally. Additionally, Diana wanted both boys to experience some of the day-to-day realities lived by the rest of the people in the country, as well as to know people from all walks of life, rather than just royalty and the aristocracy. Ken Wharfe explains, 'Diana had this desire for her sons to mix with everybody – the butlers, the kitchen staff, the maids, the dressers – so William and Harry would wander anywhere they wanted. It all became very informal and that sometimes didn't play too well with the senior royals like the Queen and even the Prince [of Wales].'

Both parents brought something equally valuable to the lives of their sons, however. While Diana was breaking down barriers, Charles was giving them the invaluable foundations for their lives as part of the royal family. Charles's godfather King Constantine II said that Charles always treated the boys like young adults and didn't force them to do anything, but explained and reasoned with them. It shouldn't be underestimated that Charles also instilled in his sons a passion and understanding for the natural world, which began in the grounds of his beloved country home, Highgrove. The property stands in a 347-acre estate, in the tiny hamlet of Doughton, Gloucestershire. Made from distinctive blonde Cotswolds stone, Highgrove was built in 1796 and Charles bought it in 1980 for over £750,000 from Maurice Macmillan, the Conservative MP and son of former Prime Minister Harold Macmillan. Highgrove lies within the country of the Beaufort Hunt, which was to play an important role in the lives of young Harry and William – helping to introduce them to country pursuits as they used to ride behind the hunt on bicycles, and in their teenage years they made friends for life with the children of fellow hunt regulars. Highgrove was also close to many of the homes of Charles's friends, including that of Andrew and Camilla Parker Bowles. At the time, Highgrove was a working farm with lots of wild parkland and no garden, but over the following decades Charles poured his heart and soul into the grounds to create something truly unique. He had hoped that Diana would help him with his vision.

Located down a long winding lane lined with blackberry bushes and oaks, and behind gates grown over with ivy, lies the impressive Georgian property where the young Harry and William would roam. It has four reception rooms, nine bedrooms, six bathrooms, a nursery wing and staff accommodation. Highgrove was a typical country retreat with a less formal style than Kensington Palace. There were heavy floor-length curtains, squashy sofas and armchairs, and overflowing bookshelves with riotous green plants and mismatched furniture, while the floor in the library was covered with Charles's papers, opened books and magazines. Nothing was to be moved. When their housekeeper Wendy Berry started working at Highgrove she was told that if there was a pen on the floor, she should hoover around it.

When he and Diana were there at the same time, Charles's dressing room was increasingly used as his bedroom and contained a patched-up childhood teddy he took everywhere with him. Diana's room was full of cuddly toys, and her bathroom had a dressing table with photographs underneath the glass top. The nursery was like another self-contained flat on the top floor, with bedrooms, bathrooms, sitting rooms, play rooms and a kitchen. When they weren't outside, the boys would spend most of their time in the nursery and ate their meals with their nanny. Barbara prepared breakfast for herself and the boys the night before, and took it up to the nursery so that none of them had to come downstairs in the morning and disturb Charles and Diana until they had been up for a few hours. The boys wore striped pyjamas, and Harry sucked his thumb. He would draw on the walls with crayons and throw his jelly and trifle around.

Highgrove was a property where a great deal of time was spent outdoors, and Charles was in his element whiling away hours outside, helping tend to the gardens, and picking herbs and vegetables for the chefs to use in their dishes. He was in his mid-to-late thirties as Harry and William were growing up, and he was happy to be expending so much time and energy on his personal project, saying he wanted to create a garden to 'feed the soul, warm the heart and delight the eye'. Although the interior of the house was cosy but fairly unremarkable, the grounds gradually became anything but. The gardens are now vast and varied: lush like a jungle in some parts and containing a species of tree that has been around since the Jurassic Period; and genteel with watercolour flower meadows in others. The Stumpery is a nook crafted entirely from tree-roots, and there is also an avenue of Alice in Wonderland-style box hedges sheared into spirals and spheres, and a wild lake watched over by a pair of crane birds made from recycled car-parts that were a gift on one African visit, while busts of those who have had an impact on Charles's life are mounted on the walls. Found growing there is the blood-red Highgrove Rose, while a tree house with a thatched roof that was built in a holly tree for Harry and William still stands today.

Highgrove is also a working farm, and much of the produce is used not just in the meals there, but in Charles's organic food range, Duchy Originals, as well as being given to a local hospice. There is a stable block with room for ten horses, a couple of farm cottages and a dairy. Charlotte potatoes, spring cabbage and Brussels sprouts are grown in the walled kitchen garden, while fruit trees in the orchards include apple, pear, plum and quince.

Charles and Diana would take the boys to Highgrove as often as possible at the weekends, and Charles would often arrive following a work engagement, while Diana would arrive later with the boys. On the Sunday she would head back to London with them while Charles would often stay another night.

To mark Harry's first birthday a set of photographs was released that had been taken by his uncle and godfather the Duke of York on board the Royal Yacht *Britannia*. In the late summer, the Queen and Prince Philip transfer to Balmoral for six weeks, while various family members and close friends come to visit and enjoy a break. Before the *Britannia* was decommissioned in 1997, a cruise through the Western Isles would kick off the holiday, and on Harry's first birthday the family were on board. Prince Andrew had recently taken up photography and on Harry's big day he took the pictures. Andrew later said, 'They were actually taken as family snaps. I was just sitting on the deck, snapping away. If there was one the princess liked and one the prince liked, then it would be used as a birthday photograph.

They weren't looking for a formal portrait.'

The 125.65-metre *Britannia* was to become very familiar to both Harry and William growing up, as the family celebrated and travelled together. The Queen was so memorably upset when the yacht was decommissioned, not only because it was the only royal palace whose interior she had created entirely herself and because it had been one of her homes since the year of her coronation, but also because of all the memories that were made by her and her family over the years.

*

Returning to London after their summer break, Charles and Diana allowed cameras into Kensington Palace to photograph and film the young Harry and William. Despite the usual sibling rivalry and rough-and-tumble between two brothers, William was actually very sweet with baby Harry, and it was clear that he was both fond of his baby brother, but also a typical bossy toddler. 'Harry!' William kept admonishing, even when Harry wasn't doing anything wrong, but also laughing at him and giving him a quick kiss on the side of the head.

Throughout the boys' early lives, they were unaware of the extent of their parents' marital issues. The irrevocable problems in Charles and Diana's relationship which stemmed from before Harry and William had been born, meant that they never knew any different. In a normal family set-up it would have been harder to disguise, but such is the nature of royal life that it helped protect the boys. Both of their parents were senior full-time members of the royal family and deeply involved with their charity work, so they would frequently be going off on engagements and attending to other commitments.

Additionally, the boys were constantly surrounded by other people – nannies, police protection officers and staff, as well as members of their family and friends. Speaking about Charles and Diana's unhappiness, and how the boys were kept from it as much as possible, Ken Wharfe says, 'The relationship was such, from such an early age, that they didn't know any different until they were older. While for Charles and Diana it was about misery, as children, Harry and William were relatively content and happy, because to the credit of both parents, their problems were obvious only to the adults who worked around them. But being royal, there was this band of helpers, always someone to take them out somewhere. Both parents did what they could without bringing in the unhappiness that they were both clearly experiencing.'

At a very young age, Harry was already displaying the daredevil characteristics that would serve him well – and not so well – in the coming years. Shortly before his second birthday he launched himself off the table at Highgrove and smashed his face on a nearby hard surface, after which he needed stitches. Even at that age he was already interested in the army, due in part to Diana's new friend James Hewitt, who was an officer in the Life Guards.

When Charles and Diana had exchanged their wedding vows, they were already both having doubts about their relationship, but Charles believed he was doing the right thing, and Diana was young and naive. Sadly, after their marriage, instead of growing closer, they grew increasingly apart and, just four years later, by the time Harry turned two in September 1986, they were sleeping in separate beds and were both looking elsewhere for affection. By the end of the year, Diana had started a relationship with James Hewitt, and Charles – who stated that he had only seen Camilla Parker Bowles at a handful of public engagements since his wedding – was now finding comfort with his former girlfriend.

Diana had met James Hewitt in the spring of 1986 at a party at St James's Palace, where she asked the proficient horseman if he would teach her to ride. In this capacity, Harry and William met James, and he became another of the many varied and interesting people around them of whom they became fond. During his six-year relationship with Diana, Hewitt told the boys stories of army life as they listened enthralled, and he also had miniature army uniforms made specially for them. Hewitt joined in pillow fights and read the young princes bedtime stories, gave them riding lessons, and took them and Diana to stay with his mother in Devon.

Later, the fact that Hewitt and Harry both had red hair prompted speculation that perhaps he was Harry's biological father, but the gossip was not only hurtful and ignorant, but completely untrue. Hewitt later stated, 'There really is no possibility that I am Harry's father. Harry was twenty months old when I first exchanged pleasantries with his mother, and past his second birthday when the affair started.' Harry had, in fact, inherited his colouring from his mother's side of the family – her sister Jane and brother Charles both had strawberry blonde hair, while her other sister Sarah is a redhead, as is her son George. Diana even used to call Harry, 'my little Spencer'.

*

Inspector Ken Wharfe joined the royal household shortly after Harry's second birthday in 1986. Police protection officers are a constant and subtle presence in the lives of the royal family. They wear tailored suits to blend into their surroundings and wear a gun in a holster in the small of their backs. Once an officer is selected for royal duty, there are extensive courses at which he or she would master specialist skills including advanced driving, first aid, physical fitness and firearms proficiency. If high enough results are attained, the prospective officer would go on the national bodyguard course, where the importance of interpersonal skills and communication is stressed: in order to properly protect the people they are guarding they have to be able to win their trust, which is why Ken Wharfe and his colleagues became such an important part of Harry and William's upbringing.

The first time Wharfe met the princes, William was trying to play the piano and Harry was pulling the stamens out of lilies. When Wharfe got the job Diana told him, 'I don't envy your job, Ken, they can be quite a handful' before adding, '... but remember, I am always around if you need me.'

Wharfe was employed by the family for the next seven years and both boys looked up to him and his colleagues. William even said once, that he didn't want to be king, he wanted to be a policeman. Wherever the boys went there were one or two protection officers, and it was essential that they build a rapport with their young charges so they would trust them.

On holiday in the Isles of Scilly, Wharfe and the other protection officers organized games of football and beach picnics. He explains of their day-to-day life, 'If their father was doing something good they would go with him, if their mother was doing something good they would go with her, and if they didn't fancy what either of them were doing, they would go and find a policeman.'

As a new face was being added to their lives, another

departed. Nanny Barnes left in January 1987, when Harry was two and a half, after her and Diana's relationship broke down beyond repair. William was upset to see her go, but Harry soon didn't remember her, and deputy Olga Powell – who Harry had also known since birth – stepped in for the next few months, before a new full-time nanny was selected.

'Olga Powell was without doubt the favourite nanny', recalls Ken Wharfe. 'She was respected by everybody within the royal household, and certainly by William and Harry, because of her experience and because of her sort of "nanny-granny" approach. She was a no-nonsense individual who had almost Edwardian codes of discipline that in today's climate you probably wouldn't get away with. I mean she would occasionally give them a smack. When he was a little older I remember one of her classic phrases to Harry was "Harry I love you, but I don't like you", because he was a nuisance. He was vibrant. But she was strong with him and I think children like that because they know where they stand.'

The next nanny to take on the job full-time was Ruth Wallace, and she stayed with the family for three years. She had a different approach. 'Ruth was a much more laissez-faire type nanny', remembers Ken Wharfe. 'A bit more fun, probably a bit wary of the Prince [of Wales]. I remember she came down to the dining table one morning wearing a pair of jeans and the Prince went completely loopy about it – jeans at the breakfast table? – that's how old-fashioned his approach was at that time.'

Harry and William stayed in touch with all of their nannies, and those who were still alive were invited to William's wedding in 2011. Sadly Ruth Wallace died in 2003, and her former charges sent a member of their household to represent them at her funeral. However, in testament to how very close they were to Olga, it was William himself who represented him and Harry (who was serving in Afghanistan) when she passed away in 2012.

Around the time that Ruth joined the team, Harry and William were allowed to start having the occasional breakfast or dinner with their parents. For Harry's third birthday in September 1987 he went to London Zoo, and the following day he started nursery. Previously at that age, royal children had always been educated at home with a governess, but Diana was determined that her boys should mix with others in their own age-group and after Charles and Diana asked around their friends, they were recommended Mrs Mynors' Nursery School, which was a short distance away from Kensington Palace. It cost £200 a term and William had also attended the school, although he had left earlier in the year. Mrs Mynors' was situated on a leafy street called Chepstow Villas near Kensington Palace, and the children who had just started were known as 'cygnets', the next year up as 'little swans' and then 'big swans'.

Dressed in blue shorts and jumper with a white shirt, and carrying his Thomas the Tank Engine bag, Harry didn't want to get out of the car at the beginning of the day, but he was soon walking with his parents and big brother William to the front of the building to meet the school's headmistress, Jane Mynors, before William tried to physically hustle him down the steps. Harry was having none of it, and made his own way down. The classroom had cut-out pictures of balloons on the walls to help the children learn the different colours, and his coat-peg was simply marked 'Harry'. Two hours later he left for the day, holding the loo-roll binoculars he'd just made in front of his eyes, looking at the photographers through them.

William would boisterously pass on his brotherly wisdom to Harry. Ken Wharfe recalls, 'William had this thing about the media. Whether Diana said in the early days to him "you have to be very careful of the photographers", I don't know, but I don't recall her ever saying that to Harry. He listened to his brother though and William would say to him, "Don't ever talk to the 'tographers, right? Don't trust the 'tographers." And Harry would be all, "Yeah, yeah, yeah." So he'd pull faces at them whereas William would pull his cap down.'

Three months later, Harry showed his impish side in front of the press when he gleefully stuck his tongue out as far as it would go to waiting photographers. They were massed outside Mrs Mynors to capture him dressed up as an elf in red woolly tights and a green tabard for his first nativity play, and when he arrived with his mother, she could be seen stifling giggles in the back of the car as he made his face, before she hauled him out.

His attitude towards the photographers would change over the coming years.

CHAPTER THREE

Behind palace walls

The royal year never deviates from its strict calendar. In the spring, the royal court moves from Buckingham Palace to Windsor Castle, and young Harry would visit with his parents and William at Easter. Diana was happy at Windsor because it was close to London, and the boys would play in the vast grounds made up of rolling green lawns, rivers and woodland filled with deer. Easter was always a big deal. The Queen would give up chocolate for Lent so there would always be a wonderful array to make up for it at the end. On Easter Sunday the family would tuck into roast lamb, and royal chef Darren McGrady recalled in his book *Eating Royally* that he would make Harry and William hand-made chocolate eggs and sugar mice.

When the young princes visited the Queen or Queen Mother they were fairly formal occasions, and Ken Wharfe recalls that Diana would say in no uncertain terms, 'I don't want any mucking about from either of you.' Harry would make a face, and she would say, 'And none of that either.'

The family would often go skiing towards the end of the season, in March or April, and Charles had always favoured the Swiss resort of Klosters, so it is there where Harry and William had their first experience of the sport. Harry was always reckless, with little or no regard for his safety. 'We were on the nursery slopes and the instructor was teaching Harry to ski,' recalls Ken Wharfe. 'He was talking to him about his stance: "Pretend you have a suitcase in one hand." "I don't have a suitcase," says Harry. "Just pretend you have a suitcase." "But then I can't go fast." "You don't need to go fast at the moment." "I want to go fast." And with that Harry was off – it was like something out of *Ski Sunday*. This was his first day. So he went down the snow, that turned into ice, that turned into grass and he ended up in a chalet at the bottom with his skis all over the place. We rushed down and I said to him, "Are you all right, Harry?" and he looked up and said, "It was good, wasn't it?" That's what Diana was like as well – instructors would be trying to guide her a certain way and she would say, "It's OK, I like skiing fast."'

Day-to-day, Diana always did the school run, unless she had a work engagement out of London, and on their way home she would often take the boys to Sainsbury's for a bag of Twiglets. Even in the city, the family would spend time outdoors in the garden whenever they could, where Diana would sunbathe, the boys would play on their swing and slide set, and Charles would barbecue salmon steaks and potatoes in foil. Their weeks were spent at Kensington Palace and at weekends they headed for fresh air, mud and the elements at Highgrove. Both boys were taught to ride from the age of two, on Shetland ponies Smokey and Trigger, by the groom Marion Cox. The boys would come in from a ride on a Sunday morning to find Diana standing by with carrots and apples that they would be allowed to carefully slice up for the guinea pigs and rabbits, while they would feed sugar lumps to the ponies.

Diana would also take the boys to the shops in nearby Tetbury or Cirencester, and they would be allowed to choose a video and some sweets. Both Harry and William loved the *Indiana Jones* films. Meanwhile, Charles would take them with him when he was out and about in the grounds, teaching them about the countryside and encouraging them to dig in their own little garden patches with the small tools he got for them – although Harry was also known to dig up the occasional ants' nest.

Charles's beloved Jack Russell, Tigger, would accompany them, and when Tigger had puppies, they kept one and called it Roo, while Charles gave Camilla one of the other puppies from the litter. The boys loved the animals of Highgrove – the dogs, ponies, guinea pigs and rabbits – but hunting, shooting and fishing also figured in their upbringing and from a young age they saw first-hand how it was possible to live off the land, they understood the process of how meat ended up on their plates. Charles raised his sons to respect and understand nature, later telling his biographer Jonathan Dimbleby that he stalks the older deer to give the younger animals a better chance of survival and therefore preventing a 'higher mortality rate in the spring when there's not enough food to go around'.

Left to their own devices, Harry and William also enjoyed playing army, and would put up blockades in the drive and dress up in their army gear, with camouflage paint on their faces, and make lunch guests and staff pay tolls. In her book *The Housekeeper's Diary*, their housekeeper Wendy Berry remembers that William would ask for 10p, but Harry would say, 'No, 20p. It's got to be 20p.' Meanwhile, on one occasion, when the royal helicopter was waiting to take Charles to an engagement, Harry attacked him from behind, but had been rolling round in the fields and was filthy, so Charles ended up – half angry half laughing – trudging back to the house to be cleaned up, exclaiming, 'Look at me! I'm absolutely covered in sheep s***!'

In the summer the family would swim in the pool and have barbecues, while the boys would drench their protection officers with long-range super-soaker water guns. A special drink at Highgrove was 'lemon refresher' – introduced to Charles by his beloved uncle Lord Mountbatten and made with sugar, lemons and Epsom Salts. There were many barbecues with the staff, which were instigated by Diana, and although Charles was uncomfortable socializing with his staff as it was not what he was used to, he realized it was important for his sons to mix with people outside of royal circles. So the boys played with new butler Paul Burrell's children and on one occasion a staff barbecue ended with protection officers jumping in the pool, followed by other employees, William, Harry and even Diana.

Although there were problems between Charles and Diana, there were occasional flashes of warmth between them, reminiscent of their early courtship, and on their seventh wedding anniversary, when Harry was four, the couple were going through a spell of getting on well, and they chased each other round the pool until they fell in, much to the boys' amusement.

Both Harry and William loved having guests, who often included Diana's side of the family. They were close to both sides, but when they were very young they spent most of their time with the children of Diana's sisters as Princess Anne's children, Peter and Zara, were a little older, and Prince Andrew's daughters,

Beatrice and Eugenie, were born later. In the late summer they would also head north to stay at Balmoral – set in the beautiful wilds of the Scottish Highlands, between the quaint towns of Braemar and Ballater. Queen Victoria and Prince Albert bought the grey stone property – which looks like a fairy-tale castle with its towers, turrets and ivy-clad walls – for £31,000 in 1852. The land has since been added to, so today it lies in 50,000 acres of vast rolling grounds and woodland that stretch as far as the eye can see.

Inside the house is a great deal of tartan decor, including tartan wallpaper, carpets and curtains, while the walls are hung with medieval swords, stags' heads, shields and paintings. Many have commented that being there is like stepping back in time, with tea poured from Queen Victoria's silver teapot and dinner served from silver salvers. There are frequent Scottish country dances in the ballroom and the male members of the family wear kilts made from Balmoral tartan (grey to represent the abundance of local lichen and purple for the heather that carpets the grounds of the estate) and the women wear white silk dresses with a tartan sash.

The vast grounds became a staple of the boys' childhood – presided over by towering hills, and thickly wooded with Caledonian Pines through which deer roamed. Much of the estate is thick with heather and full of rocky granite outcrops, winding paths, rolling moors, brooks, lakes and bridges. It is intersected by the River Dee, one of the finest rivers in the country for salmon fishing. The Queen and Prince Philip are always in residence there in the late summer. Ken Wharfe explains, 'In one year there are certain guarantees: Balmoral from July to October is one of them, and if the earth were to break up you wouldn't get them out of there until some time in the second week of October.' Numerous other members of the royal family and close family friends visit during this time, and Charles and Diana would bring the boys up for a visit every summer.

After a sustaining kedgeree breakfast, there would be morning walks in the mist, or a full-on hike through the Scottish countryside over rocks and rivers, where Charles would carry Harry on his shoulders, and all three would play hide-and-seek. The young princes would have riding lessons, and Prince Philip taught them how to fish for salmon in the River Dee, where the Queen Mother and their father were often to be found standing in the water wearing thigh-high waders. One particular spot, just five minutes from the castle kitchen, was a favourite with the princes, from which they would launch little paddle boats. They were too young for deer-stalking and game shooting, but they wanted to join in, so they were taught to shoot by the Balmoral ghillie and they would go out in the Land Rover to shoot rabbits. According to royal chef Darren McGrady their kills were brought back, cleaned, cooked, deboned and given to the corgis for dinner. There was game on the menu most days because of all the shooting. The finer cuts were marinated and Prince Philip barbecued them in the evenings. The second best were cut up, braised in red wine and used in stews, served with mashed potato, and the third grade ones were ground into sausages.

There would be numerous picnics, and if the weather was bad, a roaring fire was involved – a lot of the living at Balmoral was done outside. Most of the family's favourite picnic and barbecue spots would be based next to one of the grounds' simple enclosed shelters, or at the Honka House, a plain wooden hut-type building, which was a gift to the Queen and Prince Philip for their twenty-fifth wedding anniversary from the people of Finland, and containing a sitting room, kitchen, bathroom and sauna. A favourite Balmoral dessert was cheesecake made with crème de menthe, topped with a crumbled mint Aero. The boys, however, favoured queen of puddings made with sponge, jam and soft meringue. The Queen would wash up afterwards, before they all headed back to the house.

However, for all the family fun, Diana felt isolated at Balmoral, and it was here that the twelve-year age gap between her and Charles was most apparent. She was in her early-to-mid twenties during Harry's early childhood, and she missed the vibrancy and variety that their London life offered. While the rest of the family enjoyed walking and hunting as they were lashed by the elements, and relished bundling up for meals outside, Diana simply felt cold, wet and disconnected. She didn't enjoy country pursuits, and was also suffering from an eating disorder, so the days involving shooting and heavy meals were difficult for her. Additionally, her emotional nature and desire to break with tradition had caused friction in the family. However, she would take Harry and William to the nearby Craigendarroch Country Club for a swim, and would let the nanny go in the evenings so that she could spend suppertime with her boys.

During the summer holidays, Harry and William would also go to stay with Diana's mother in her whitewashed farmhouse in Seil, near Oban, Argyllshire on the west coast of Scotland. Seil is a tiny, rugged island that is joined to the mainland by a bridge which, in summer, is covered in foxgloves. There, they would go mackerel fishing, lobster potting, and as the sea was right on their doorstep, sailing. Diana would wash and iron everyone's clothes and do the dishes, and the boys absolutely loved it, although Diana loved it even more – getting back to basics, where everything was stripped down and simple, and in the company of her mother.

When they were a little older, Harry and William would go on exotic holidays with their parents, but when they were very small the only other summer breaks they took aside from their jaunts to Scotland, were to the Scilly Isles off the tip of Cornwall, or to the Spanish island of Majorca. In the Scilly Isles, Charles and Diana favoured the island of Tresco with its seals, flowers and sandy beaches. Meanwhile, in Majorca, they would stay with King Juan Carlos of Spain at his cliff-top palace overlooking the capital, Palma. Occasionally throughout the year they would visit the Queen's Norfolk residence Sandringham where they would often spend time on nearby Holkham Beach learning to fly kites and building sandcastles.

*

Royal Christmases always used to take place in Windsor Castle, but for most of Harry's childhood the year would certainly always end in Sandringham, as it still does now. The red-brick property was built in 1870 and is set in 20,000 acres of land that includes farms, woodland, beautiful gardens and orchards. Christmas trees are grown on the estate, so there are always a few impressive specimens on display inside during the festive season. The house itself has been the private home to four generations of British monarchs, and it is where the Queen's father King George VI had passed away. Royal Christmases had previously been held at Windsor Castle, but they switched to Sandringham when Harry was young. Staff decorate the Norfolk spruce, felled from the estate, with Queen Victoria's angels and baubles, but the Queen herself adds the tinsel and the star on top when she arrives a few days later. Royal Christmases are very traditional. The rest of the family arrive on Christmas Eve – Harry and William would have already received their card from the Queen, which she would always sign 'Granny and Gramps' – and they would gather in the White Drawing Room for afternoon tea while the boys headed to the nursery with their cousins Peter and Zara, who were seven and three years older than Harry respectively. The children always got their own Christmas cake – one year it had Father Christmas bursting out of the top, another year it featured Sonic the Hedgehog.

The whole family would then gather later in the White Drawing Room to open their presents on Christmas Eve, according to German tradition. As the name suggests, the room has a light, pale colour scheme, with cream silk Victorian sofas dotted with cushions embroidered by the Queen's grandmother, Queen Mary. Trompe l'œil ceiling panels are painted to look like windows showing pale blue sky with pheasants and doves around the edges. There is no overhead lighting, just small wall-mounted lamps, so at night, with the fires burning in two fireplaces and the fairylights on the tree, the rooms would sparkle as the lights reflected off the mirrored doors, glass cabinets of treasures and the floor-to-ceiling picture windows.

Each member of the family would have their own table covered with a white linen tablecloth. Prince Philip always started proceedings and then everyone would dive in, in what Princess Margaret's son Viscount Linley has described as 'total uproar'. Harry and William's presents would usually comprise athletic equipment, games, Nintendos, electronic toys, books and crafts. One year the boys received super-soaker water guns and sneaked into the kitchen to ambush the chefs. The adults often received simple or joke presents – the Queen was enthusiastic about a casserole dish she received one year, and Prince Charles collects toilet seats. One Christmas when Harry was older, he gave the Queen an apron, and a shower cap with 'ain't life a bitch' written on it.

When the family awoke on Christmas Day there would be stockings filled with fruit and treats at the end of each bed. After a quick breakfast they would always head out to church for the 11 a.m. service at St Mary Magdalene, which is on the Sandringham estate and dates back to the early sixteenth century. It has a silver pulpit, memorials on the walls to the Queen's ancestors, a jewelled bible and a Florentine marble font. Yet the church is small and intimate: the rest of the congregation is made up of people who regularly attend the church throughout the year, and they apply to attend the Christmas Day service in the autumn so they can pass security checks. The silver altar is decorated with holly from the estate, and there is a tree in the nave. For the collection, the Queen, Philip and Charles give an ironed ten-pound note, which is folded so that the Queen's head faces out.

Outside, after the service, people gathered from all around to pay their respects, and the family would mingle with them before taking a brisk walk back to the house and a change into formal-wear for lunch in the dining room. This is a more dark and cosy room, with walls painted in Braemar green – a light pistachio green – with walnut and mahogany panelling, and Spanish tapestries on the walls. This room would be lit by two trees, flickering with coloured lights. At 1.15 p.m., the family would sit down around the mahogany table that can seat up to twenty-four. For Christmas Day it would be set with silver candelabra, fresh flowers, and silver pheasants and partridges. Drinks were taken from crystal-wear engraved with EIIR, and lunch often eaten off the Copeland white and blue dinner service bearing George V and Mary's monogram. Menus were in French, as they always are when the Queen is hosting, whether it is a private event or state occasion. Christmas lunch for the royal family was similar to that of most families up and down the country – Norfolk turkey, herb stuffing, sausages wrapped in bacon, Brussels sprouts with braised chestnuts, glazed carrots, roasted and mashed potatoes, cranberry sauce, bread sauce and gravy. There was also salad, and sometimes samphire – a plant that grows in marshes near the sea nearby – according to chef Darren McGrady tasting like 'salty asparagus'. Dessert was two Christmas puddings with brandy sauce, and mince pies with brandy butter. These would be followed by a cheese board that always included a huge Stilton, sent every year from Harrods, and then coffee, while the sideboards were loaded with chocolates and sweets. The family pulled bespoke crackers, read jokes and wore the paper hats.

Lunch was done and dusted in an hour-and-a-half so they could all sit and watch the Queen's speech at 3 p.m. in the Saloon, the royal family's sitting room. The room is cream with earthy neutral tones, huge Brussels tapestries on the walls, bountiful plants, antique rugs, and always a jigsaw puzzle on the go on a side table. The television was usually stored in a cabinet but was brought out and they would watch in silence before the Duke of Edinburgh raised a glass of brandy – to 'Her Majesty the Queen'.

Afterwards it was time to relax, and some members of the family would go for a walk. At 5 p.m. tea was served on the sideboard – sandwiches, yule logs, Christmas cake, brandy snaps and mince pies. In the evening, the TV would be off and they played games – the Queen loves charades and is an excellent mimic, as is Harry. Over the years they also played Trivial Pursuit and Monopoly, and one year the Who Wants to be a Millionaire?

board game. After which a screen and projector might be set up in the ballroom for those who wanted to watch a film. Suitably grand for its name, the ballroom has mottled gold-and-silver leaf wallpaper that looks almost like military camouflage, while the walls are hung with a grisly-looking collection of knives and swords from India and the Far East that had been given to Queen Victoria's son Edward.

The Boxing Day shoot was and is as much a part of the tradition as the events of Christmas Day, and the boys liked to get involved as soon as they were allowed. The shoot was always organized by Prince Philip and took place over the muddy fields on the estate, targeting partridge, woodcock, quail, duck and pheasant. The family have lunch in a plain wooden hut surrounded by trees in the heart of the estate. They would cluster around a paraffin heater to cook sausages, and heat soups while they drank spirits and tea. They would also have venison stew, mashed potatoes, sautéed cabbage and fried plum pudding with brandy butter prepared for them, along with Harry's favourite, treacle tarts.

No one was ever in any doubt as to what to buy for Harry, as he always made his desires clear to all concerned. He was obsessed with the army and wanting to be a soldier, and his favourite toys included a set of lead soldiers and a miniature Panzer tank. When James Hewitt had miniature army uniforms made for him and his brother, Harry wore his to threads and pleaded for another one. 'He always, always wanted to be a soldier', recalls Ken Wharfe. 'I never saw him out of his khaki uniform. And he was obsessed with guns. He would say, "Can we see your gun, Ken?" "No!" we'd reply, "You only take a gun out of its holster if you intend to use it."'

CHAPTER FOUR

A bearskin rug, a bottle of cochineal and a snooker ball

Harry was interested in every aspect of the army, and because of his privileged position, many of his wishes were granted. 'When Diana was seeing James Hewitt, there were endless opportunities for Harry to play the young soldier,' recalls Ken Wharfe. 'He and William had unlimited access to all the army's technology and camps out in Wiltshire that were made available with Hewitt's contacts. He didn't abuse it though, and Harry was always very appreciative. As soon as they got back Diana would force him and William to write thank-you letters.'

Diana and Charles both indulged Harry's love of the military and, after he watched the film *Zulu* for the first time, he asked his father about the battle of Rorke's Drift in which around 150 British and Colonial soldiers defeated thousands of Zulu warriors in 1879. He would also ask the members of the royal family about their experiences in the military, especially his uncle and godfather Prince Andrew, who was a navy pilot and fought in the Falklands War. Andrew would tell his nephews war stories and Harry, in particular, was mesmerized. Later, when James Hewitt went to serve in the Gulf War, Diana would anxiously watch the news with Harry by her side.

Shortly before his fourth birthday, in 1988, Harry went to Great Ormond Street Hospital for an emergency hernia operation. By this time Charles and Diana were leading increasingly separate lives, illustrated by the fact that Charles was on a painting holiday in Italy with friends. He and Diana had completely different interests, and completely different social groups, people of their own age, who shared their interests. Charles was friends with Charles and Patti Palmer-Tomkinson, and an old Cambridge University contemporary Hugh van Cutsem, a pedigree bloodstock breeder, along with his wife Emilie. Charles would have the Parker Bowles and the Palmer-Tomkinsons over for supper, and often on such occasions Diana would make her excuses and retire early, taking a tray of food in her room. Her friends included David Waterhouse who was a captain in the Household Cavalry, banker Philip Dunne, her old flatmate Carolyn Bartholomew and her husband, and heiress Catherine Soames.

Charles and Diana did not spend much time together, and their cars often passed each other outside Highgrove, with one leaving as the other arrived. The boys had been used to this since they were born, and so when they were young they didn't question it. Additionally, whenever they went on holiday, it was never usually just the four of them, there would always be other people present. Whether it was Balmoral, or Majorca, or summer cruises, there would always be nannies and protection officers around and, as they got a little older, the boys would also be allowed to take school friends along as well. It was only when

Diana took the boys to visit her mother on Seil that they went without an entourage of people.

Harry and William have always been incredibly close. Ken Wharfe says, 'They were joined at the base of the spine in some ways.' However, from an early age they had their own personalities. 'Harry would be the more mischievous and had a "don't care" attitude, whereas William was more reserved,' explains Ken. 'I remember we took some go-karts down to Highgrove one weekend. William took charge of it and said "I'm going to make a track round the back drive that goes through Papa's vegetable patch," and Harry said, "Why don't we make it come across here, and it will cut up all the grass!" William said, "We can't do that because Papa will go mad." Harry brushed it off: "It doesn't matter about that!"'

Ken continues, 'William was likeable, but capable of being quite sly. He would choose to attack from behind as a child, whereas Harry would always try to grab your nuts.' They would have the usual brotherly tussles, and Ken recalls, 'William could be quite demonstrative and sometimes bullying towards Harry, but Harry didn't really have a problem with that because he could fight his own corner. Very often he was on top of the game and had to be remonstrated by the nannies and pulled off.' Even though he was the youngest, and had, growing up, been treated as less important by some members of staff, Harry certainly had no problem in asserting his presence.

As Harry turned five in September 1989, he joined William at Wetherby pre-prep school, just a few streets from Mrs Mynors in nearby Notting Hill. He started a week late because he had been ill with a virus, but headmistress Miss Blair-Turner was there to greet him when he was better, as he arrived in his grey uniform with scarlet trim, which was only available from Harrods. The school takes boys from the age of four-and-a-half to nine.

Over the next year, there were further changes. Ruth Wallace, who had been the boys' nanny for the past three years, left and was replaced by Jessie Webb. Along with long-standing deputy Olga Powell, Jessie remained with the boys until they no longer needed a nanny, but like Olga, she remained close to them. While Olga passed away in 2012, Jessie was asked by William and his wife Kate to be nanny to their son George. However, her first royal job didn't get off to a good start. 'Jessie was an interesting character,' recalls Ken Wharfe. 'She was a good nanny, but more of a fun person. They used to play Jessie up because she wasn't really their type and she would come and knock on my door and say "Ken, can you have a word with them, they're being very naughty," and I would have to be very careful about overstepping the boundaries but of course I tried to help. I would say, "Harry, what's going on, mate?" "I don't like Jessie," he'd say. "Well you'd better get to like her, OK? I gather you've been rude to her." "Well, I said something." "What did you say?" "I told her she should lose weight." "Well that's not very nice, Harry, is it?"'

He would later apologize to Jessie because he was under strict instructions from Diana to do so. Wharfe recalls that Diana or Olga would say to Harry whenever he misbehaved, 'Go and say sorry, or you won't be able to watch television.' However, Harry would even give the strictest nanny Olga the runaround. 'If she reprimanded him he would say, "Go to your room, Olga!"' remembers Wharfe. 'She was in her sixties then and would start chasing him through this labyrinth of corridors until eventually she would have to give up and then she would be like, "Ooh, I'll kill him!"'

Diana gave her the authority to give both boys a slap around the back of the legs if they misbehaved, but Harry would get away with his cheeky behaviour because he was so well liked. His godmother, Diana's friend Carolyn Bartholomew, said when he was young that he was, 'The most affectionate, demonstrative and huggable little boy.' While Wharfe says, 'He was like a friendly Labrador dog who liked everybody – if someone took him off and gave him some food he would go – Harry was like that too.'

Just four days before Harry's sixth birthday, William was enrolled at Ludgrove School, where he was a boarder. He would return home some weekends, but during the week it was just Harry and his mother, or Harry and his father now. 'That was something he enjoyed, I think,' says Wharfe. 'Instead of having to share things, he had everything to himself. He was always moving around. He would wander into the kitchen and say, "Any chance I can help make something?" The chef would say, "What would you like to make?" And he'd ask, "What's Mummy having?" So they'd give him an egg to whip, then he would get bored and bugger off.'

He was always pushing boundaries, illustrated by an anecdote from Wharfe about his time at school. 'He was a rogue at Wetherby,' Wharfe recalls. The music master there, Robert Pritchard, used to play the piano for school assembly. When Harry was around six, and one day sat on the floor beside his teacher at the piano, he kept pulling the teacher's trouser leg and saying, "Mr Pritchard! Mr Pritchard!" Robert was hissing, "Shut up, Harry,"' recalls Ken. '"Mr Pritchard! Mr Pritchard!" "Sssh, stop it, Harry." "Mr Pritchard! Mr Pritchard!" "What is it, Harry?" "I can see your willy, Mr Pritchard!" Robert felt duty-bound to tell the headmistress and she took me to one side and said, "What shall we do about this?" I said, "That's Harry. I wouldn't worry about it. I'll tell his mother and she will find it absolutely hilarious. The less we do with this the better." So I told Diana and she was in absolute hysterics – arched-back laughter. Two days later we were back at the school and we ran into Robert, and Diana went up to him laughing and said "Ah, Mr Pritchard, I hear my son saw your willy the other day!" Poor old Robert went as red as anything and we all had a good old laugh about it.'

Would any other pupil have got away with putting a teacher in such an uncomfortable position? It seems unlikely. But this new generation of the royal family were in unchartered territory. Diana wanted the boys to have a 'normal' upbringing. She encouraged the boys to mix with members of staff in all the royal properties, and ensured they went to nursery instead of being home-schooled with governesses. She gave them pocket money and took them on the tube and the bus. She also took them to the London Dungeon, the zoo, the cinema and for a McDonald's. At Christmas, she queued with all the other parents so the boys could meet Father Christmas at Selfridges. However, their lives were still not normal by anyone else's standards. They lived in castles and palaces, were constantly surrounded by policemen and staff, there were photographers waiting outside, they were chauffeured to nursery at the age of three, while Harry's playthings included a baby grand piano and a toy railway set that had been a present from London Underground.

The notion of 'normality' as defined by members of the royal family is tricky to pin down. If Diana wanted to take the princes to Marks & Spencer to buy a snack they were happy to be 'normal', but when the boys got away with high jinks that wouldn't perhaps be tolerated were they not royal, then they were protected by their status. In this way 'normality' appeared to be a somewhat moveable notion, which was really not the same for the rest of the country. Ken Wharfe believes that both boys were aware of their station from a young age, 'I think Harry was about six when he made a classic statement. William would have been eight, and he said to William, "You'll be King, I won't, so I can do what I want!" At the age of six!'

There were some things Harry perhaps got away with because he was a prince, but there were other things he got away with more because of what his parents were going through. 'We went to stay at someone's house after a wedding,' Ken Wharfe recalls. 'Diana came down in the morning and said "Have you seen Harry?" I said, "No, I'll go and find him." It was late spring and at the front of this house there was a big circular garden full of daffodils – and Harry had picked all of them. I said, "Harry, what have you done?" "They were nearly dying, Ken," he said to me. "Me and my friend were just tidying them up …" William wouldn't have done that. When I told her, Diana laughed. No one did anything about it.' It seems Diana and Charles already had enough on their plates – their marriage had broken down beyond repair, and there was worse to come.

As they grew up, Harry and William became more aware of their parents' relationship breaking down. William was older and it affected him more. He would sometimes find his mother crying, although Ken Wharfe says, 'She would make fun of it and turn it into something else. Harry was interested in having a laugh.'

Their minds were taken off whatever was happening at home by heading out to the homes of family friends and losing themselves in a gaggle of local children. One of their favourite places was Anmer Hall, the Norfolk home of Prince Charles's Cambridge friend Hugh van Cutsem and his wife Emilie (and now soon to be the country home of William, Kate and Prince

George). The van Cutsems had four sons, and the princes grew up around them, with William later selecting William van Cutsem to be one of Prince George's godfathers. Another of their favourite places to spend time was at the home of the Prince of Wales's friends Simon and Claire Tomlinson, who ran the Beaufort Polo Club. The couple had known William and Harry from birth and had three young children who were a little older than the two princes.

Claire, a former professional polo player, recalls, 'I liked them to know that they could come any time they liked. Of course, it was very difficult for the boys when everything blew up at home. It was a pretty difficult life for them, so it was just nice for them to know that there was somewhere they could relax, knowing that everything they said wouldn't be repeated. They grew up among friends, and wanted to be treated like everybody else. I think that's what their parents wanted as well. They just got on with their life and that was nice for them.'

The boys would muck in with all of the other local children, riding different kinds of horses, practising with sticks and playing bicycle polo before progressing on to the real thing. 'When you're small and you start riding, you're not going to ride a dragon,' explains Claire. 'You have something suitable, and always the idea is to get children confident in their horses, and then it's great fun.'

William and Harry had been riding for years, having been taught on Shetland ponies at Highgrove, but as they got older, they also enjoyed learning new skills at their local polo club. At the Tomlinsons', they got to learn and play under the protection of the couple, who helped ensure that the boys were treated exactly the same as the other children there. 'Harry was very appreciative,' Claire remembers. 'He would often visit if his parents weren't at home, and he was always very polite. I think he started playing polo because he was able to, and once you start playing polo, I promise you, it's very addictive – you can't stop because it's such a fantastic game. It involves the riding, the hand-eye coordination, the team play, and the relationship you build with the horse as well. There are some people who are quite tough with the horses and they don't get the best out of them. Harry appreciates the horses.'

*

When Harry turned seven Diana threw him a party at Kensington Palace with Sarah, Duchess of York, her daughters Beatrice and Eugenie, and lots of friends. The following month, on their first formal trip as a family to Canada, one of the most recognizable pictures of Diana with her boys was taken. Charles and Diana had been touring Canada on their own, and had a joyful reunion with William and Harry on the Royal Yacht *Britannia* in Toronto. While pictures of an overjoyed Diana, with her arms held wide as her sons ran towards her, were beamed around the world, the pictures that weren't were of Charles greeting them just seconds later.

In March 1992, the family headed to the Austrian Alps for a skiing holiday. Previously, Charles and Diana had always favoured the Swiss resort of Klosters, however, in 1988 the royal party had been struck by tragedy when an avalanche hit and killed one of their group. Diana and Sarah, Duchess of York, had been back at the chalet but Prince Charles narrowly escaped death, while his friend Major Hugh Lindsay was killed, and Patti Palmer-Tomkinson was seriously injured. Afterwards, Diana insisted upon never returning to Klosters and so from that point the family had favoured the Austrian resort of Lech. It was here that they heard the news that Diana's father Earl Spencer had died of a heart attack. He had recently been admitted to hospital with pneumonia but he was only sixty-eight years old and his death was unexpected. Diana was devastated. It was Harry and William's first real experience of death, but Ken Wharfe explains, 'The boys were kept out of it. I don't recall any emotion from them. They actually didn't have a great deal of contact with Lord Spencer. I remember a few visits up to Althorp and he was a charming man – he was a generous typical granddad figure and loved William and Harry, but contact was minimal. Diana broke the news to them, but at that age they just wanted to stay on skiing and having fun, and so that is what happened.'

The young princes stayed on with their nanny, Olga, and two protection officers, however it wasn't so straightforward for their parents. 'Initially the princess didn't want to travel back with the prince, and he wanted to stay skiing with his children,' recalls Ken Wharfe. 'But there was a sense of duty. In the end, she saw sense and realized for face they needed to go back to London together.'

Soon afterwards – without Charles – Diana took Harry and William, her mother, her sisters and their children, her brother Charles and his new wife Victoria, to Necker in the Caribbean. Virgin Chief Executive Richard Branson had bought the tropical island in the 1980s and offered Diana a trip there. The Great House, a large Balinese villa, is described by Ken Wharfe as a 'cross between the lobby of a luxury hotel and a Surrey barn conversion', while the resort is surrounded by four exclusive beaches, with the use of speedboats and jet skis. Harry and William decided that if the paparazzi found them, they would attack them with water balloons. Sir Richard Branson's manager had bought three giant catapults and hundreds of water balloons, and when the inevitable happened, the princes set them up to bombard the press pack. Diana thought it was hilarious. However, she found it less so when the boys got into a fight.

Ken Wharfe says it was the most angry he had ever seen Diana at Harry, 'Branson had a full-scale snooker table, but the boys were too young to play,' he recalls. 'One day Harry had had an argument with William. William was taunting Harry, saying "You can't play because you're not big enough, so it's banned for you – it's only for us big boys." "Oh no, it isn't!" says Harry. William said, "You can't even reach the table." So what does Harry do? He gets a snooker ball and whips it down the table and it smacks into William's fingers. William bursts into tears and runs off to Diana, "Harry's just thrown a snooker ball at me." Diana came down to find out what happened but I told her that William had been taunting him, saying he was too small. She wasn't pleased about it and she told him not to do it again.'

Wharfe adds that Harry the daredevil was always up to something, 'You had to keep an eye on him. There was an infinity pool in Necker and the water just dribbled over the edge. Of course, Harry would go and stand right on the edge. He was always pushing the boundaries. That was never the case with William, he would never have done that. He would be the first to say to his mother, "Oh, Harry's done such-and-such again."'

Harry was never the boy to sit still with colouring books and puzzles, however, he would need constant stimulation. On one visit to Lech, Harry couldn't resist a particularly intriguing item. The son of the owner of the hotel was a hunter and the hotel walls were covered in his kills. Ken Wharfe remembers, 'On the floor of this annexe, next to the swimming pool, was a great

Grizzly Bear, and one afternoon Harry picked this bear up and put it on – we found him on the back stairs.'

He would also come looking for a fight – literally. Wharfe recalls, 'Harry would come and knock on my door and say, "Any chance of a fight, Ken?" Then I'd go and beat him up for half an hour.' He would see how far he could go, and Wharfe also recalls, 'Occasionally, when we were at Highgrove and someone would have a glass of wine with dinner, Harry would say, "Is that wine, Ken? Can I have a sip?" and we'd say "No" and he would try his luck and say, "Papa lets me have a sip sometimes". "No!"'

He also poured red food colouring acquired from the Kensington Palace kitchen into Wharfe's bath when he had stepped out of the room leaving the taps running, and even went missing on one occasion. 'He came to me and said, "Ken, can you give me a job? Can I do a radio job?" I said, "Why don't you go and see Aunt Jane?" I rang and said, "I'm sending him down, just give me a call when you send him back and the CCTV will pick him up." He never turned up. So I called him up on the radio and said "Where are you?" and he said, "Just a moment … I'm outside Tower … Tower Records." I said "Stay there!" You would never have got William doing something like that. Harry had a real sense of adventure, he would do anything, he was up for anything. What he did lack, was someone sitting him down and saying "Look there's certain things you can do, and certain things you can't."'

CHAPTER FIVE

Struggling at school

In June 1992 Andrew Morton's book *Diana – Her True Story* was published. It was a shocking account of life behind palace walls and inside Diana's marriage, which made public her battle with bulimia and Charles's relationship with Camilla. Diana claimed publicly she did not collaborate on the book, but had in fact contributed tape-recorded interviews, which she passed to her friend Dr James Colthurst, who, with her knowledge, passed them on to the author. While the outside world reeled at the details, Harry and William were unaware of the book's contents and their impact until they were older.

That summer, Diana was understandably in bad spirits when they cruised around the Caribbean. Charles was friends with Greek shipping entrepreneur John Latsis and was often loaned his luxurious yacht, the *Alexander*. The 122-metre vessel had a gilded interior, with gold taps and crystal chandeliers, and contained fourteen suites, along with a disco bar, cinema, Turkish baths and a swimming pool with wave runners and water skis.

Diana talked of being airlifted off, but she was persuaded to stay for the sake of her boys, while Harry was typically daredevil when he leaped thirty feet into the sea, daring William to join him.

No sooner were they back in the country than Diana was back in the headlines. This time, taped conversations between the princess and PR executive James Gilbey had been run in the *Sun*. By this time, Diana had broken up with James Hewitt, but although she and Gilbey were clearly close, Diana later denied they had a physical relationship. However, they were very familiar and Gilbey used his pet name for Diana 'Squidge' or 'Squidgy' so many times that the release of the tapes became known as 'Squidgygate'. The telephone conversations had been recorded when Diana was at Kensington Palace and Gilbey was in Oxfordshire, and had been picked up by an amateur radio operator in Oxford.

Despite their mother's private life spilling into the papers, Ken Wharfe explains that, because of their unusual circumstances, Harry and William were kept away from it all and were unaware of what was being said in the press. 'It wasn't like a normal home, where kids are always aware of what their parents are doing,' he states. 'If there was ever any sort of crisis they would be farmed off to friends, or the nanny would take them off, or a policeman would take them off. Anything that happened they were conveniently repositioned away from the problem.'

Additionally, although William was older, he was already at boarding school where there were no newspapers, and TV was monitored. It was a pre-internet age and so he was protected from a lot of what was going on and the matters that were being reported.

*

Shortly after Harry turned eight in September 1992, he joined his brother as a boarder at Ludgrove. The rural surroundings meant that it would be a secluded place for Harry to learn and grow, away from the public eye, and since the school was formerly a farm, it was set among rolling green fields and woodland, which meant plenty of space for the boys to play. The old milking parlour now houses a ceramics, art and carpentry block, and pupils would make dens and camps in the woods. In the summer they would sleep out occasionally on the golf course and have sing-songs around the camp fire.

Ludgrove is a family-run school and during Harry's time there the headmaster was Gerald Barber, who had taken up the role from his father Alan, while Gerald's son Simon is headmaster there today. The school provided a safe, supportive and inspiring environment, while encouraging the boys to grow into confident and self-sufficient teenagers. Just as when William had started, two years earlier, the doors of Harry's dormitory were reinforced, and bullet-proof windows were added, while protection officers were always nearby, but apart from that he was treated the same as any other pupil.

When he started at Ludgrove he was driven to the school by Charles and Diana, arriving with his trunk of clothes and tuck box of other personal effects. In the same way as all the other boys' parents, his parents were asked not to come back, or to call, as this would make things harder for him to settle in. Until his first exeat (weekend home) a few weeks later, they were advised just to write.

The school was divided into houses where each group of boys lived – undertaking classes and sports activities elsewhere in the grounds. The boys were grouped together in houses to encourage their community spirit, and there would be competitions and sporting events where the houses would indulge in some friendly rivalry. Each house was looked after by a housemaster – a kind of parent figure, who would build a close relationship with the boys, mentoring them and overseeing their development, and act as a main point of contact for the parents. Each house also had a matron, who looked after the domestic side of life – from laundry to ailments to a lost teddy bear – and she was assisted by a number of under-matrons. All teachers were simply referred to as 'Sir' or 'Ma'am', but nicknamed 'beaks', while the under-matrons, who were usually younger women, were referred to as 'Miss' followed by their surname.

The dormitories slept around twelve boys, and each had a cast-iron bed with a bedside table alongside. The floors were wooden parquet and there were spectacular bay windows overlooking the grounds. On the boys' first day their things were unpacked by the under-matrons into large cupboards in the main corridor, and the young women would sort the clothes every few days. The boy's trunk contained his clothes, while his tuck box was fitted with a lock, and would be used to store personal items, ranging from spare stationery, to letters from home, sweets, CD player, CDs and magazines.

Harry's day would begin when the matron came to draw the curtains at 7.15 a.m., and the boys would roll out of bed to brush their teeth, wash, dress and head downstairs for breakfast. There was no fixed uniform. The boys wore corduroy trousers with a shirt, jumper and blue or brown tie. In the summer, they wore aertex shirts, but no shorts, trousers only – they were, after all, young gentlemen. Vitamins were dished out in the morning, after which the boys would line up outside the refectory, sitting at their tables at 7.45. The pupils from the first three years would sit in the main refectory – wood-panelled and hung with pictures of former pupils – while those from the final two years ate in the conservatory. Cereal was already in the bowl in front of them – Weetabix, Rice Krispies or cornflakes. Kippers and scrambled eggs were also available.

After breakfast there would follow three lessons, then a break with milk and cookies, then two lessons, followed by lunch, then another two lessons followed by sports. At weekends and on Wednesdays there were just sports, which was Harry's favourite part of school. At every meal prayers were said in Latin or Greek by the headmaster. Lunch would be something hot like one of Harry's favourites – cottage pie; while in the evening there was more variation with pizza and pasta available. After supper there was time for private reading and homework, and in their free time the boys would head to the reading room with big comfy chairs and chess or to the games room where they could play board games, table-tennis and billiards.

Exeat would fall every three weeks, so most weekends the boys remained at Ludgrove, where they would participate in lots of sports and tended to the gardens. The school grounds are full of trees, so they could climb, build dens, and they also played a game particular to Ludgrove called 'tie chase', in which they were grouped into large teams and one boy would tuck a tie into his shorts and the object was to catch this boy by pulling out the tie. There was always chapel on a Sunday, and afterwards the boys wrote letters home to their parents. After they had written them they had to show them to the headmaster so that he could ensure each letter was long enough – two sides of paper – and that it was tidy. The headmaster would not read them, and each boy would seal the letter himself. Sunday lunch was often cold cuts, salad and a baked potato, and a drink called Creamola Foam was popular with all the boys – it came powdered in a tin and fizzed when mixed with water. Boys would keep a tin in their tuck box although they were only allowed it on Sundays. On Sunday afternoons Gerald Barber would show old classic war movies in the refectory on a screen above the fireplace – including one of Gerald's favourites, *The Heroes of Telemark*.

For his first exeat Harry went to Norfolk with his father, and in the November of his first year he went to Highgrove with his mother. Wharfe remembered, 'I sensed going to Ludgrove was a turning point for Harry. He left behind his childish behaviour and there was real-life stuff at Ludgrove. He took to it better than William. He struggled educationally but there were so many extra-curricular activities, which he loved. He grew up there.'

*

Just three months after Harry started at the school, Diana drove to Ludgrove to tell him and William that she and Charles were separating. It had been a particularly terrible year for the couple, and the Queen had finally given her permission for them to take this step. Once the boys had been told, it was announced in parliament by Prime Minister John Major on 9 December 1992, who stated, 'It is announced from Buckingham Palace that, with regret, the Prince and Princess of Wales have decided to separate. Their Royal Highnesses have no plans to divorce and their constitutional positions are unaffected. This decision has been reached amicably and they will both continue to participate fully in the upbringing of their children.'

Because there was no intention to divorce at this stage, Diana would retain her royal status and lifestyle. Ken Wharfe says Diana was very careful in the way that she told the boys, and that they weren't surprised by the news, 'Her delivery was such that it wasn't going to change their relationship with their mother or their father. They had known no different. I don't think they were upset because I don't think it changed their life. I asked Diana what they were like and she said they were fine – they just wanted to go and play again.'

Now the boys were away at school, they were protected by their environment – again, there were no newspapers, TV was kept to a minimum, and it was before internet access, so they were able simply to be distracted by studies, friends, sports and games. However, they spent their first Christmas Day apart from their mother. Tradition required that they spend the festive period with their father and the Queen at Sandringham, while Diana spent Christmas with her family at Althorp for the first time since she had been married. Sarah, Duchess of York, was out of royal favour since she had been photographed on holiday in the South of France with her financial advisor, John Bryan, kissing her feet, and she and Prince Andrew had also separated. But she was permitted to stay at a smaller property, Wood Farm, on the Sandringham estate with her mother and sister, so she could see her daughters over the festive season. Prince Andrew drove over to visit her on Christmas morning with Beatrice and Eugenie, while Charles drove over with William and Harry on Boxing Day.

In the winter of 1992 all of Charles and Diana's staff and possessions were divided up. Diana remained in Kensington Palace while Charles moved into York House in a wing of St James's Palace. One of the oldest palaces in London, it was built on the remains of a hospital for female lepers (the hospital of St James) and bought by Henry VIII. It was the official royal residence of the monarch before Buckingham Palace, and it was where Harry and William returned with their father on weekends and holidays from school when they were in London. Diana had Kensington Palace redecorated after Charles left. The decor was was light and bright, retaining some of the antiques and original paintings, but was now also hung with modern pictures. She was to spend most of her time with the boys in her sitting room, which had a big squashy toy hippo on the floor. Her bedroom was redecorated in pastels with scented candles, and lots of cushions with white lace and frills. There was a chaise at the foot of the bed, harking back to her childhood bed, it was covered in fluffy toys. Her dressing room was covered in children's pictures from the charities with which she was affiliated. She kept a few memories of Charles in Kensington Palace, but he, on the other hand, wiped all trace of her from Highgrove, and had it redecorated by Robert Kime, in a more conservative, traditional feel – darker and richer, with upholstered furniture and heavy red curtains.

After spending Christmas with their father and his side of the family, they welcomed in the New Year with their mother on the island Nevis in the Caribbean. Compared to some of its luxurious neighbours, at the time Nevis was more of a rugged tropical island. It was small and covered in rainforest, but edged with pristine beaches. Along with one of Diana's friends and her children, they stayed at the Montpelier Plantation Inn, located on an old sugar plantation, set in sixteen acres and comprised of sixteen private chalets. It was surrounded by secluded gardens and stone terraces. In the mornings, the hotel staff would make them a packed lunch picnic, and they would go off for the day in a pickup truck, with the boys' surf boards sticking out the back, to one of the deserted beaches nearby, such as Indian Castle Beach or Pinney's Beach. One day Harry instigated the capturing of twelve giant toads and William, the hotel owners' children and the police protection officers joined in. Then they had a race, but unfortunately the toads all hopped off in different directions.

Back in the UK, reality bit again for Harry and William's parents when the *Mirror* ran the transcript of a conversation between Charles and Camilla. It was never determined who made the recordings, but Charles and Camilla worked out that it was in fact a compilation of a few conversations they had had over several months around Christmas 1989 – shortly before Diana's leaked conversation with James Gilbey. Like Diana's, they weren't made public until some time after. The press focused on the racier parts of the recording, but the content was more interesting in what it said about the couple's relationship. This was not the hearts and flowers of young love, but the real love of two people who knew each other very well, and that ran deep. In both the Charles/Camilla and Diana/James tapes, the non-royal party was supportive, sympathetic, affectionate and flattering. It was a shame that Charles and Diana couldn't provide this for each other, but the sad fact was, right from the beginning, they had never been suited.

Harry and William both made friends at Ludgrove with whom they are still friends to this day. One was Jake Warren, whose family home is Highclere Castle, which doubles as TV's Downton Abbey. He was Diana's godson, and his father runs the Queen's stud farm. Harry also became good friends with Henry van Straubenzee, while William was already friends with Henry's older brother, Thomas. There was a link to their mother with this friendship also, as Diana had previously been a nanny to their cousin.

Once he had settled in, Harry enjoyed the camaraderie of school. He found it hard to concentrate in class, however, and while William knuckled down, Harry wasn't as strong academically and relied on his boundary-pushing and cheeky sense of humour to win favour. He later said while reflecting on studying: 'Exams were always a nightmare, but anything like kicking a ball around, or playing PlayStation or flying, I genuinely find it easier than walking sometimes!'

Meanwhile, Ken Wharfe said, 'He wasn't the brightest academically. He wasn't stupid, but there were too many distractions for him. He was always getting told off. If there was fun to be had, he would do that rather than work. His concentration threshold was not brilliant. He did find school difficult. I think he found school a bit of a chore.' Harry later told the *Sun* columnist Jeremy Clarkson that he suffered from dyslexia, and although it has never officially been confirmed, it appears to be backed up by his statements about struggling with written exams – whether at school, or later when he was studying to fly helicopters.

Outside of school, Harry and William's lives with each parent were quite different. At Kensington Palace, Diana was in many ways like any other young divorcee. She was still just thirty, and felt as if she was making up for lost time, reclaiming her youth and making new friends. She was interested in New Age practices and befriended psychics, astrologers and New Age healers. She had Kensington Palace 'cleansed' after Charles left, and visited seers, read psychic magazines and cast runes. She was also interested in organic food and read up on aromatherapy and reflexology. She socialized with celebrities such as Cleo Rocos, Kenny Everett and Freddie Mercury. She went to the Harbour Club to work out, played tennis, had lunch at San Lorenzo. Meanwhile, her work took her to Zimbabwe with the Red

Cross to raise awareness of the plight of refugees, and a leprosy hospital in Kathmandu. Through her work for homeless charity Centrepoint, she took William and Harry to homeless shelters, where Harry played cards with the rough sleepers there. Both Harry and William later spoke of their mother coming back from her trips and telling them about what she had been doing with such infectious enthusiasm that it has stayed with them into their adult lives.

Diana also started stripping away from herself the formality and tradition of the royal way of life, there was no French cuisine or game on her menus. When the boys were back from school, instead of being waited on, Diana asked chef Darren McGrady to leave everything on the sideboard 'all in' – dinner and dessert – so they wouldn't be disturbed by staff in between courses. A typical lunch was roast pork, corn on the cob and potato skins, followed by banana flan or pear and banana crumble. At that time Diana was still good friends with Sarah, Duchess of York, and she would come for lunch with Beatrice and Eugenie, when there would be jam pennies (jam sandwiches cut into circles, a favourite of the Queen) and home-made chocolate chip cookies. They also loved a cake made from bashed-up rich tea biscuits and lots of melted chocolate, which William was to choose as his informal wedding cake for the evening reception after his wedding in 2011.

The boys would drift in and out of the kitchen looking for snacks and would sometimes help make Diana's favourite – stuffed aubergine. That year they went skiing at Lech again, but it was the first time they had been since Charles and Diana's separation, and interest in the family had reached fever pitch. One reporter was asking ten-year-old William to say a few words, when Ken Wharfe stepped in, stating that the prince was too young to give an interview, 'I went to restrain him,' recalls Wharfe. 'I slipped, then he slipped and fell in the snow. The next thing I hear is Harry saying, "Watch your back, Ken", as this guy gets up and runs towards me before others restrain him. This was Harry, he wanted to be involved. It didn't matter how he was involved, it was just his character. It's an impetuous move on his part – "I've got to do something". He doesn't always engage the brain before moving forward. He doesn't think of repercussions.'

Harry was, however, on best behaviour when his mother, as Colonel-in-Chief of the Light Dragoons, took him with her to Germany to visit the regiment. As she undertook her official duties she told those she met, 'Harry is really into soldiers at the moment.' Ever since the uniform James Hewitt had made for him had fallen apart, Harry had wanted another, but he didn't get one until he was presented with one in Germany. Once he was dressed in it, and his face had been smeared with camouflage paint, he clambered into a Scimitar tank, as machine guns rattled out empty rounds, and drove through multi-coloured smoke. He was hooked.

While he was able to grill his father and Uncle Andrew about military life, his mother too appreciated his growing passion and used her contacts to allow Harry to realize some of his army dreams when he was young, including visiting the Metropolitan Police Firearms Training Unit, in Lippitts Hill. Ken Wharfe remembers, 'He was allowed to shoot a gun, and he was good at it. Suddenly he's realizing a boyhood dream. He's a soldier holding a gun. He was seven or eight at the time. Both William and Harry were taught to respect guns and were taught gun safety from a very young age.'

When the boys were with their father they spent a lot of time with Peter and Zara Phillips, who had also been through the pain of their parents' divorce. They also spent time with their little cousins Beatrice and Eugenie. Additionally, a new face was added to their lives, as Charles employed twenty-eight-year-old Tiggy Legge-Bourke to be a nanny/companion. They grew to adore her, especially Harry. Her real name was Alexandra, and her mother Shan and aunt Victoria had both been ladies-in-waiting to Princess Anne, therefore Tiggy had been known to Charles for some time. After leaving school she took a nursery teacher training course at the St Nicholas Montessori Centre in London. She then taught for a year before leaving to set up her own nursery school, Mrs Tiggywinkles, in Battersea, South London. She would call the children her 'Tiggywigs', which is how she got her nickname. Tiggy was originally an assistant to Charles's private secretary and moved across to the nanny/ companion role after Charles and Diana's separation.

Like the royal family, Tiggy was sporty and outdoorsy – into skiing, riding, fishing and shooting. She was tactile, boisterous and good fun, and said of her royal charges, 'I give them what they need at this age – fresh air, a rifle and a horse. She [Diana] gives them a tennis racket and a bucket of popcorn at the movies.' Diana was understandably annoyed by her comments, but it wasn't to be the last time Diana was irritated by her sons' new companion, as Tiggy was later to refer to the boys as 'my babies'. Diana also didn't like the fact that Tiggy smoked in front of her children. Harry and William, however, loved her, and grew to regard her as a big sister. She loved them and cared for them when they were staying with Charles, but was also raucous and would let them get away with things that a parent might not.

Harry turned nine in September 1993, and he and William settled into their new routine. Both parents were happier. They spent alternate exeats with Charles and Diana, riding horses and following the hunt when they were with their father and when they came to stay with their mother they would play tennis at the gym with her, ride BMX bikes, go go-karting. Diana would also take them to WHSmith to buy comics and then to the cinema and sometimes for a McDonald's afterwards. Diana would dress them in caps and disguise herself in a brown wig. Traditionally, the royal family don't carry cash but Diana thought it was important for the boys to understand how the rest of the world survived earning salaries and handling cash, so they would know the value of it. They also wanted to be able to pay their own way when they were out with their friends. In the evening, they would watch action films like *Rambo*, or something with Arnold Schwarzenegger, or they would play Nintendo.

In July 1994 came the ITV documentary *Charles: the Private Man, the Public Role*. It was the first time Charles had admitted his adultery with Camilla, when being interviewed by his biographer Jonathan Dimbleby. 'Did you try to be faithful and honourable to your wife when you took on the vows of marriage?' Dimbleby asked. 'Yes. Until it became irretrievably broken down, us both having tried.'

The book, *The Prince of Wales: An Intimate Portrait*, followed in the autumn and, unfortunately for Charles, the fascinating detail and different aspects of his character were overlooked, and information about his childhood was taken out of context and cast the Queen and Duke of Edinburgh in a poor light. Andrew Parker Bowles formally brought an end to his marriage, and soon afterwards married his long-term girlfriend. Shortly after the Charles biography was published, James Hewitt's book *Princess in Love* came out, detailing his romance with Diana.

It was an extremely turbulent time for Charles and Diana, and the War of the Wales's was in full swing. Even though they had now separated, they were still always in the news.

Harry turned ten in September 1994, and the following year Charles took him to visit the Royal Engineers, the corps who had been involved at Rorke's Drift. The Wales's first public trip as a quartet since the separation was on 7 May 1995, to Hyde Park to commemorate the fiftieth anniversary of VE Day. Three months later, in August, the boys joined the Queen, Charles and the rest of the royal family to commemorate the fiftieth anniversary of VJD, and they were excited to be allowed to stay on board the *Britannia* and watch the fly-past and massive fireworks display.

Shortly after his eleventh birthday, in November 1995, Diana took part in a *Panorama* interview with Martin Bashir, which, for the nation, was as shocking in its candour as it was riveting, as she spoke unfavourably about aspects of her life in the royal family. Afterwards, the Queen agreed for the Wales's divorce to be pushed through and Diana's HRH title was removed, although she was still considered to be a member of the royal family and would continue to live at Kensington Palace. She stripped away even more accoutrements of royal life, shedding staff and pruning back the charities she worked for. Diana claimed that she didn't want to be going to assorted balls and events which would take her away from the actual work she wanted to be doing. She retained just six charities: Centrepoint, the English National Ballet, Great Ormond Street Children's Hospital, the Leprosy Mission, the National AIDS Trust and the Royal Marsden NHS Trust. She took the boys to The Passage, a homeless shelter near Vauxhall Bridge in London, where they chatted with the volunteers and played cards with the homeless.

*

It was all change personally for the princess as well as this was the year that she met Hasnat Khan, a Pakistani-born heart surgeon, whom she met while visiting a friend at the Royal Brompton Hospital. It was a low-key relationship, but it was to continue for the next two years and the couple fell in love. 'Diana was madly in love with Hasnat Khan and wanted to marry him,' her friend Jemima Khan told *Vanity Fair*. 'Even if it meant living in Pakistan.'

Diana was much happier – she felt freer and more in control of her own life. She also stopped speaking to Sarah, Duchess of York, who had released her autobiography in which she said she caught a verruca from Diana after borrowing her shoes.

Life continued for both boys as normal – they were both away at school and so managed to avoid a lot of their parents' problems. They were able to enjoy their time away from school with each parent, experiencing two different lifestyles. In April 1997, at the age of twelve, Harry was photographed hanging out of the back of a Land Rover shooting rabbits as Tiggy drove; and in June William invited Tiggy to the traditional Eton summer picnic instead of his parents and she was photographed smoking while she was with him. Diana was incandescent that Tiggy seemed such a bad influence. Both boys adored Tiggy, however, and while they were in the care of their father she went everywhere with them – half term and summer holidays, skiing, Sandringham and Balmoral. She took them to pony clubs, gymkhanas, shows, polo lessons, and tea with their friends, and she accompanied them rabbit shooting and driving after the hunt.

As the summer of 1997 approached, Harry should have been leaving Ludgrove. Diana really wanted Harry to follow William to Eton, and said, 'If he doesn't go there, everyone will think he is stupid.' However, he had been struggling at school, and was kept back for a year. So when they broke for summer, Harry already knew he would be returning to Ludgrove again in the autumn, and looked forward to spending the first part of the summer in the south of France with William and Diana, before he and his brother joined his father and the rest of the royal family for their annual break in Balmoral.

Harrods owner Mohamed Al Fayed had invited Diana and the boys on holiday. They were relatively new acquaintances, but he had donated generously to Diana's charities, and when he made the offer for her, Harry and William to join him and his family at their home in the south of France, before spending some time on his new yacht, she decided to accept. She was at the time coming to the end of her romance with Hasnat Khan – she was still serious about their relationship but he could not live with the constant scrutiny that came with being involved with the most famous woman in the world. She liked the idea of spending the summer in the Mediterranean.

CHAPTER SIX

'Mummy'

On 11 July 1997 Diana, Harry and William arrived in the south of France on Mohamed Al Fayed's private jet. The Al Fayeds' summer home, Villa Castel Ste-Thérèse, is set in the mountains over St Tropez amid ten acres of land. With a private beach, swimming pools and a private disco, it was perfect for all ages of the party, although feisty Harry and Al Fayed's son Omar, who was a similar age, argued over bedrooms.

They were soon joined by Al Fayed's forty-two-year-old son Dodi, who had worked as a producer on the film *Chariots of Fire* and in the marketing department of his father's store, Harrods. Dodi hired a disco for the princess and her sons to dance in private, and they all went to Le Renaissance Bistro, followed by an amusement park where they rode the dodgems. The boys also raced around the bay on jet-skis.

The group then transferred to Mohamed Al Fayed's yacht to cruise the Mediterranean for a few days. Al Fayed had just spent £15 million on the 63.5-metre *Jonikal*, which was all light golden blonde wood and contemporary interior, with cream furnishings. The group were followed by the ever-present paparazzi, some of whom chartered a helicopter to fly overhead. Diana was angry and ended up taking a boat out to complain to the photographers. 'William is freaked out!' she shouted. 'My sons are always urging me to live abroad to be less in the public eye and maybe that's what I should do – go and live abroad.'

On 20 July, the boys said goodbye to their mother and the Al Fayeds, and flew back to England for the Queen Mother's ninety-seventh birthday lunch at Clarence House. They then embarked on the last ever cruise round the Western Isles of Scotland on the *Britannia* with their father and the royal family, going on to their annual stay in Balmoral.

Diana continued her summer holiday, cruising round the Greek islands with her friend Rosa Monckton for the next month, before flying back to London. It was then that she ended her relationship with Dr Hasnat Khan, many of her friends believing that she was tired of his reticence to commit to her in the way she wanted. She then spent time in Sardinia with Dodi on the *Jonikal*, before arriving in Paris on 30 August with her new beau for a brief stopover. They had been swarmed over by the paparazzi since they set foot in the French capital, and when they left the Paris Ritz that night, bound for an apartment owned by Dodi's father, they left by the back exit while a decoy left from the front. They were soon spotted, however, and the paparazzi gave chase to the black Mercedes driven by Mohamed Al Fayed's driver, Henri Paul.

Charles was informed of his ex-wife's car crash in the Pont de l'Alma tunnel minutes after it happened around 11.30 p.m. on Saturday 30 August. It was reported in Katie Nicholls' book

William and Harry that he walked down the corridor at Balmoral in shock to break the news to his parents, after having been told that Dodi was dead and that Diana was in a critical condition. Shortly after 3 a.m. the next day, Charles was informed by the British Embassy in Paris that Diana had passed away. She had sustained terrible chest and head injuries, and lost consciousness very soon after the crash. She was treated in the wreckage of the Mercedes and taken to the Pitié Salpêtrière Hospital, four miles away, where surgeons fought for a further two hours to save her life. Charles woke William at 7.15, and together they went to tell Harry.

Until this point, the nearest person to the boys who had passed away was their maternal grandfather, Earl Spencer, but at that time they had been cushioned by their parents, their youth and their lack of contact with him. This loss was raw and all-consuming – Harry was twelve and William fifteen and this time there was no escape because their mother was their entire reality. Faith is an integral part of being a member of the royal family, and William said he wanted to 'talk to Mummy', so he and Harry were driven to Crathie Kirk nearby, where the Queen attends church when she is in residence. Crowds gathered to offer condolences – everyone wanted to reach out and comfort the two boys. Their cousin Peter Phillips flew to Balmoral and Tiggy Legge-Bourke was already there as she had flown up the previous day to escort Harry and William down to London. Harry would not leave her side, and asked in the church, 'Are you sure Mummy is dead?' because there was no mention of her in the service.

Years later, when William became patron of the charity Child Bereavement UK, he said, 'Losing a close family member is one of the hardest experiences anyone can ever endure. Never being able to say the word "Mummy" again in your life sounds like a small thing. However, for many, including me, it is now just a word.'

New Prime Minister Tony Blair made a television appearance to pay tribute to Diana, and one of the terms he used for her was to be associated with her forever after. Looking harrowed, he stood before the assembled press to speak, 'I feel like everyone else in this country today – utterly devastated … People everywhere, not just here in Britain but everywhere … they loved her. They regarded her as one of the people. She was the people's princess and that's how she will remain in our hearts and in our memories forever.'

Charles flew to Paris to accompany Diana's body back to the UK, arriving back at 7 p.m. on 31 August. The coffin was draped in the royal standard, the Queens' official flag, and was met by Tony Blair. As the hearse made its way to the royal chapel in London traffic stopped all the way along the route, and people bowed their heads as the vehicle passed. As Charles then returned to Balmoral to be with his sons, members of the public held a candle-lit vigil outside Kensington Palace.

No one in the country had ever experienced anything like this before. Diana was home-grown but world famous, a beautiful, glamorous mother who broke the rules and made it her mission to care for those who had been forgotten by others. She was just thirty-six years old. As the days slowly passed, the people of Great Britain didn't know what to do with their grief, and as well as piling flowers upon flowers at the royal palaces, many felt a sense of anger that the flag hadn't been lowered at Buckingham Palace. Flags were flown half-mast at the Queen's residences at Holyrood House and Windsor Castle, but not at Buckingham Palace. There, the flag was never under any circumstances flown at half-mast, however the British public began to see this as a symbol of the royal family's lack of caring. (In fact it was after the public reaction to Diana's death that the Queen ordered a break with royal protocol and the Union flag was flown at half-mast over the Palace on the day of Diana's funeral.) There was also anger that the Queen hadn't spoken publicly in tribute to Diana. People wanted to see emotion. The Queen believed the family's bereavement was a private matter.

The Queen's priority was, of course, her vulnerable grandsons. Among the hundreds of acres of wild craggy moorland, lochs and rivers that they had known since birth, they were surrounded by their closest family. They went fishing and riding. The Queen was in regular contact with Tony Blair, as a state funeral was being planned. Charles and his sons went out to Crathie Kirk to look at the flowers that had been laid there and read some of the messages. Harry held his father's hand and knelt to read the tributes at the gates of Balmoral. 'Look at this one, Papa.' 'Read this one.' The sight of them together softened the public mood. The following day the Queen – who had returned to London – addressed the nation in a television broadcast. Apart from her regular Christmas broadcast this was only the second time she had done so in her thirty-five-year reign – the first was during the Gulf War. This time she stated simply, 'What I say to you now, as your Queen and as a grandmother, I say from my heart. First, I want to pay tribute to Diana myself. She was an exceptional and gifted human being. In good times and bad, she never lost her capacity to smile and laugh, nor to inspire others with her warmth and kindness. I admired and respected her – for her energy and commitment to others, and especially for her devotion to her two boys. This week at Balmoral we have all been trying to help William and Harry come to terms with the devastating loss that they and the rest of us have suffered … I for one believe that there are lessons to be drawn from her life and from the extraordinary and moving reaction to her death.' She and the Duke of Edinburgh also walked among the floral tributes at Buckingham Palace.

Charles, Harry and William broke with royal protocol by flying back from Balmoral together. Ordinarily, because they were the first, second and third in line to the throne, they were unable to fly together in case the plane crashed and the future of the royal family was wiped out. However, these were unusual circumstances: the boys were in shock and they needed to be with their father. The Spencers had wanted a small private funeral and the Queen agreed, however Charles wanted a full royal funeral at Westminster Abbey and, as public reaction intensified, the Spencers agreed with Charles.

On the day of the funeral, the gun carriage carrying Diana's coffin made its way from the Chapel Royal to Westminster Abbey. Walking behind were the Duke of Edinburgh, Prince William, Earl Spencer, Prince Harry and the Prince of Wales. On that terrible day, Charles Spencer walked between William and Harry and later recounted, 'It was just awful. It was something I would never wish on anyone. You could not look on either side, you were just walking through a tunnel of grief and it was a very odd feeling because you could feel the depth of despair coming in waves on either side. I still have nightmares about that. I can hear the bridles and all the metalwork on the horses and their hooves and the wailing of the crowd. I have never been in such a nightmarish place in my life.'

Despite the oceans of flowers that swept the front of Kensington Palace, Buckingham Palace and the Pont de l'Alma Tunnel in Paris, all eyes were on the small posy of white freesias from Harry and William that sat on her coffin, along with the letter that was sealed in a white envelope with 'Mummy' written in Harry's handwriting. Guests, including American first lady Hillary Clinton, had flown in from all over the world to pay their respects, along with Tony Blair, Margaret Thatcher, John Major, and Hollywood stars Tom Cruise, Nicole Kidman and Steven Spielberg. The Spencer family and Mohamed Al Fayed were among the last to arrive but, according to protocol, the royal family were the very last into the Abbey. As the bells of Big Ben pealed 11 a.m., Diana's gun carriage reached the West Door and eight Welsh guardsmen carried the coffin as they slow-marched down the nave.

The cameras were off Harry and William inside the abbey, but Harry broke down when his mother's coffin passed and Charles cuddled him close, while his older brother put a comforting hand on his shoulder. After the National Anthem, Diana's favourite hymn 'I vow to thee my country' was sung, and it was followed by a rendition of 'Libera Me' from Verdi's Requiem, which visibly moved Prince Charles. Prime Minister Tony Blair read 1 *Corinthians*, 13, and Diana's friend Elton John sang his re-worked version of 'Candle in the Wind'.

Many of those mourning the princess had felt fogged and numb with grief, but when Diana's brother Charles Spencer read the eulogy it was a sharp, sobering strike that pierced the sadness. It was an emotional address, in which he also expressed direct anger at the press and veiled anger towards the royal family. He honoured his sister as, 'Someone with a natural nobility who was classless and who proved in the last year that she needed no royal title to continue to generate her particular brand of magic.' He continued, 'Of all the ironies about Diana, perhaps the greatest was this – a girl given the name of the ancient goddess of hunting was, in the end, the most hunted person of the modern age. She would want us today to pledge ourselves to protecting her beloved boys William and Harry from a similar fate and I do this here, Diana, on your behalf. We will not allow them to suffer the anguish that used regularly to drive you to tearful despair. On behalf of your mother and sisters, I pledge that we, your blood family, will do all we can to continue the imaginative way in which you were steering these two exceptional young men so that their souls are not simply immersed by duty and tradition but can sing openly as you planned. We fully respect the heritage into which they have been born and will always respect and encourage them in their royal role but we, like you, recognize the need for them to experience as many different aspects of life as possible to arm them spiritually and emotionally for the years ahead. I know you would have expected nothing less from us.'

Many believed it wasn't perhaps the right place for such anger, but the public reaction was overwhelming. Ken Wharfe was a guest inside the Abbey and recalls, 'What happened next was extraordinary, and something that only those inside the Abbey that day will ever fully appreciate. Lord Spencer's loving yet devastating address was followed by a stunned silence. Then a sound like a distant shower of rain swept into the Abbey, seeping in through the walls, rolling on and on. It poured towards us like a wave, gradually reaching a crescendo. At first I was not sure what it was … It took me a couple of seconds to realize that it was the sound of people clapping.' Most of the congregation joined in, including William, Harry and Charles. The Queen, Prince Philip and the Queen Mother did not.

Afterwards, Diana's body was buried at Althorp, and Charles took Harry and William back to Highgrove. Tiggy was there to get them through not only the next few days, but the immeasurable ones after that. She was there when they walked around Kensington Palace, deciding on which of their mother's personal things they would like to take away to remember her by, and after that it was decided the best thing for them was normality. Just two days after the funeral, Tiggy took them out to follow the Beaufort Hunt on foot. When they arrived, the hunt master paid his respects to the boys and was thanked by William. Both boys were back at school just four days after the funeral. Harry was quieter and less boisterous when he returned. He didn't used to care about studying but he needed to pass his common entrance to Eton, and worked hard in his final year. Only five days after he returned to school it was his thirteenth birthday. Diana's sister Lady Sarah McCorquodale visited him, bringing the PlayStation that Diana had bought for him in Paris.

Charles had been planning on introducing Camilla to the wider world that September, but the public perception of the royal family was confused, emotional and coloured by Diana's death. The people grieved for her as if they had known her personally – and they also took her side against Charles. Diana had publicly blamed Camilla for the breakup of her marriage, and therefore so did much of the rest of the country. For a while, Camilla stopped going to Highgrove, and Charles would spend every weekend with his sons. It was thanks to him that another important figure came into their lives after Diana died. Mark Dyer was an ex-Welsh Guards officer who was employed as a kind of male version of Tiggy – a cool, no-nonsense, hard-living adventurer who was a bit like a big brother to the boys. He and Tiggy were old friends and were both devoted to the boys, and they to them. Mark had been equerry to Charles when the boys were younger and Charles asked if he could come back to help them through this difficult period.

To boost Harry's spirits, on his half-term break in November 1997, Charles took him and one of his school friends to Africa.

Tiggy also went along, and while Charles undertook official duties, Tiggy took Harry and his friend on safari in Botswana. They all then met up in Pretoria, South Africa, where Harry was introduced to Nelson Mandela, and met the Spice Girls, who were at the peak of their fame, and were there to perform a concert. Harry held hands with Victoria Beckham and Emma Bunton, and couldn't stop grinning – shortly afterwards stating that the day he met them was the best day of his life. Harry then fulfilled a very personal, longer-held ambition when Charles took him to Rorke's Drift, which he had first learned about in the film *Zulu*.

For anyone with a love of the outdoors, the mind-bogglingly vast wilds of Africa can be overwhelming. With its huge sky and swift, flaming sunsets, wide open spaces that have remained virtually unchanged for centuries, and its red earth trodden by so many incredible creatures – it can be hard to take in. For a British child, these animals are the stuff of wildlife parks and television programmes presented by Sir David Attenborough – to see elephants lumbering through the bush, huge-maned lions prowling malevolently on heavy paws, or a giraffe with legs splayed at a watering hole, is almost like seeing dinosaurs come back to life. Wild and untamed, Africa got under Harry's skin, and it was the beginning of a lifelong love affair with the continent where he would one day declare he wanted to live.

CHAPTER SEVEN

After-hours and under-age

During Easter 1998, Charles made the first steps to pave the way to Camilla becoming accepted as his partner, so that they could marry. He was in a very strange position; he was a forty-nine-year-old man who would one day be king, with a long-term partner whom everyone knew about, but they could not be seen together officially. The first step was to introduce Camilla as his partner to Harry and William. The boys had known her when they were growing up, but not in the capacity of their father's partner. They had also known her children, Tom and Laura, since they were very young, as Tom is Charles's godson. Tom is ten years older than Harry, and Laura is six years older, but they hadn't seen them for some time. The path was made smoother by bringing the children together, and Tom and Laura were invited to stay in Birkhall, along with a few others, to break the ice. Harry was used to mixing with all age groups, and many of his father's friends' children were older, so although he was just thirteen, and Laura was nineteen, and Tom twenty-three, they found a way to connect.

Around this time, William and Harry started planning a surprise birthday party for Charles, who was turning fifty in November. They wanted to invite their father's godchildren and their parents and, obviously, that meant Camilla would be invited. William wanted to meet with Camilla first in private, which he did at Highgrove. Harry took it in his stride when he met with her shortly after.

The following summer, after they had all been re-acquainted for a year, Charles and his sons went sailing on the yacht the *Alexander* with Camilla and her children. It was their first holiday with both families, although William and Harry also took friends with them.

Tiggy once again came under attack when the boys went abseiling under her watch down the side of the Grwyne-Fawr dam in Monmouthshire, Wales, that autumn. Both princes took turns, but William was already at the bottom when Harry was on his way down and was photographed by a passer-by. When the picture was printed in a newspaper, there was a furore because neither of the boys was wearing protective headgear. Charles was horrified, but Harry defended Tiggy, who was like a big sister to him and she kept her job.

There was a church service to mark the first anniversary of Diana's death. At first, William did not want to attend because of the press attention, but Harry persuaded him to go and he agreed on one condition: that the service would mark an end of the public mourning for Diana. Harry later stated in an interview with American television channel NBC to publicize the Diana Memorial Concert, 'When she passed away … there was never any sort of lull. There was never that sort of peace and

Above: The Prince and Princess of Wales, Prince Charles and Princess Diana, pose for a family portrait with their sons, Prince William (right) and Prince Harry, at Kensington Palace in 1984.

Left: Prince William giggles as his baby brother tries his hand at the piano in Kensington Palace in 1985.

Above left: The brothers in their much loved military uniforms at Highgrove in 1986.
Above right: A royal cuddle while on holiday in Majorca in 1987.
Below left: Still holidaying in Majorca, a cheeky shot of the young prince.
Below right: Her Majesty The Queen with the two Princes, 1987.

Above: Favourite nanny Olga Powell hugs young Prince Harry as they watch
a Polo match in Windsor, 1987.
Below left: Embarking on his first day at Wetherby School, Prince Harry looks up
at his big brother, 11 September 1989.
Below right: Prince Harry as a pageboy at his uncle's wedding, seen here with his
cousins Eleanor and Alexander Fellowes, September 1989.

Above: Young Harry (left) with the royal family at the Trooping of the Colour, Buckingham Palace, 1989.
Below: An early start for the young prince as he 'rides out' with the Beaufort Hunt foxhounds in 1993.

Above: Diana, Princess of Wales, Harry and William on a visit to Thorpe Park amusement park in 1993.
Right: With F1 driver David Coulthard at Silverstone, Prince Harry looks on with his cousin, fellow red-head, George McCorquodale (right).

The Action Prince: military training seems to have been on his mind throughout his childhood. *Left:* Young Prince Harry with his beloved Super Soaker. *Below left:* On a visit to Germany in 1993. *Below:* As a serving soldier in Afghanistan.

Left: The young Prince holds his father's hand while looking at the floral tributes laid outside the gates of Balmoral Castle after the death of his mother, Diana, Princess of Wales, September 1997. *Below*: Diana's funeral, 6 September 1997.

Above: With 'Tiggy' Legge-Bourke, nanny to the two princes, at Cirencester Park Polo Club.
Left: With Baby (Emma Bunton) and Posh (Victoria Beckham) at a Spice Girls concert in Johannesburg, November 1997.

quiet for any of us. Her face was always splattered on the paper the whole time.'

William went over the wording of a statement that was then read out by a member of their father's team at the photo-call when Harry joined him at Eton. It read: 'They believe their mother would want people to move on – because she would have known that constant reminders of her death can create nothing but pain to those she left behind. They therefore hope very much that their mother and her memory will now finally be able to rest in peace.'

*

Having taken his common entrance exam in History, Science, English, French, RE, Geography and Maths to attend Eton, Harry passed – and he knew that his mother would have been thrilled. In September 1998, just days before his fourteenth birthday, he started at Eton.

Eton has become one of the most famous educational establishments in Britain, and yet only a privileged few have studied there. It has produced eighteen British prime ministers, including David Cameron, and some of the most talented actors around today including Damian Lewis, Tom Hiddleston and Eddie Redmayne. Harry's uncles on both sides – Charles Spencer and Prince Edward – had both attended the college, as well as Camilla's son, Tom Parker Bowles, and he already would know a few familiar faces, including brother William, some of William's friends, and other boys he knew from Ludgrove. Charles had been miserable during his school years at Gordonstoun and he and Diana wanted William and Harry to have a more enjoyable time in their education.

The college itself was founded in 1440 by Henry VI and fees start at £10,327 a term. The school is interwoven with the chocolate-box town of the same name, and many of the town's buildings are owned by the school, which means that in order to get to lessons, boys dash up and down the quaint little paths and alleyways lined with wooden-timbered Tudor houses. The college's buildings include three theatres, two concert halls and two libraries.

Scholars (called 'Collagers') inhabit the College and eat in the most magnificent room in the school, the rest of the boys ('Oppidans') are scattered between twenty-four boarding houses through the town. There are no dorms – from day one every boy had a study bedroom, which changes every year as he moves up the school. Harry joined Manor House, with William, which is the most prestigious of the twenty-five houses, situated next to the library, and the 'burning bush', an elaborate wrought-iron street lamp that stands at the centre of the school.

His housemaster was Dr Andrew Gailey, who was referred to as 'Sir', and the matron was Elizabeth Heathcote, who was referred to as 'Ma'am'. There were also maids who cleaned and tidied their rooms. After having tea with his housemaster and his wife Shauna, along with the other boys starting that year, William showed Harry round. There was a games room with pool table, and a common room with two overstuffed sofas, plastic chairs and a TV. There were trophies, medals and pictures of school plays all over the walls.

After the familiar security of Ludgrove, and the strong and supportive relationship he had developed with headmaster Gerald Barber, Eton was a much bigger, more complicated place. The timetable changed from week to week and there was a uniform: for lessons the boys wear school dress – black tailcoat, waistcoat, a stiff white collar with paper tie and pinstriped trousers. There was a lot of slang specific to Eton, from abracadabra (the basic timetable) to wet bobs (rowers). When they were older, on Sundays, the pupils would walk over the bridge and get a McDonald's and see action movies at the cinema on the high street, but they had to be sure to be back before their 8.15 p.m. curfew.

Harry made friends for life around this time, including among them Tom Inskip, the son of a Beaufort Hunt field master, and Guy Pelly, whom he also met through the hunt. Guy and Tom – or 'Skippy' as he was known – were two friends who were to become as party-loving and exuberant as Harry and, later, fingers of blame were wagged at them. However, Harry was perfectly capable of getting into trouble by himself – although it was better to do it alongside close friends who cared about him, and would stick by him.

Harry wasn't as academic as William, but was becoming known for his cheeky sense of humour. He would hide behind curtains in class, only emerging at the end of the lesson; he would balance a book above a door so that it fell on the teacher's head. He also jumped out on William from behind a tree during a cross-country race, shouting, 'Can I have your autograph?' Which prompted an earbashing from William for losing him a place among the front-runners. Harry later said, 'I know that when I was at school, sport was the best thing, being stuck in a classroom wasn't.' By the end of the first year he was behind in every subject.

In April 1999 at the age of fifteen, Harry returned to Africa – this time with William, Tiggy and Mark Dyer – for a ten-day safari to Botswana. They visited the Moremi Game Reserve, where they stayed in thatched huts, and also traversed the swampy Okavango Delta, where Harry would one day return with his first love. By the end of the year, Tiggy left Prince Charles's service when she got married. Harry was already showing signs that his youthful boisterousness was turning into adolescent high jinks when, at her wedding, he was said to have swallowed a goldfish from one of the table decorations.

The boys would often take summer holidays to Rock in Cornwall, staying in a private house with their friends the van Straubenzees. Known as the 'Kensington of Cornwall' and 'Sloane Square-on-sea', after the well-known moneyed areas of London, every summer Rock would see a massive influx of public school teens, all drinking, surfing, kissing and hanging out. The Oystercatcher bar was one of their favourite haunts. During the day they played French cricket, and learned to surf on Polzeath Beach, and later they partied into the night after beach barbecues. Harry is remembered at the Mariners gastropub in Rock for squashing his nose against the glass to make girls laugh as they walked past.

The fun-loving prince was photographed by Lord Snowdon for his sixteenth birthday, and a few months later chipped his thumb playing football. Although he didn't have a way with academia, he threw himself into physical activity. He was House Captain of Games, and represented his school in rugby, cricket and polo. At sixteen he played the Eton wall game. Harry was in the Oppidans and they played against the Collagers. Two teams of ten players form a bully or scrum and are forbidden from using their hands to free the ball from a mass of bodies.

Harry had always been a joker. He liked to push boundaries, and he was fearless. When alcohol is added to that kind of mix, the results are going to be interesting at best – disastrous at worst. This was the year that Harry's partying was becoming a little too public. He was smoking Marlboro reds and drinking in the pubs around Highgrove. A favourite watering hole was the local Rattlebone Inn. William and Harry would be joined by their cousins Peter and Zara, who lived nearby with their mother Princess Anne in Gatcombe Park. It was reported there were lock-ins, and members of their group smoked marijuana outside.

By the summer of 2001 Charles was often away tending to royal duties, or at Birkhall with Camilla, and William was on his gap year, which left Harry with the free run of Highgrove. Additionally, on a summer holiday to Marbella he stayed out drinking until 6 a.m. and trashed the golf course when he drove around it in a buggy, hacking at the grass with a golf club as if it were a polo stick. In the past he had been disciplined by Diana or Olga Powell but now he was treated by his family as a young man and given a certain amount of freedom.

He and William also turned the cellars of Highgrove into a hangout: Club H consisted of two adjoining rooms, with high arched ceilings, one of which was used as more of a club and was painted black, with a state-of-the-art sound system and two large cream sofas. There was a portrait of their ancestor the Duke of Windsor hanging in the loo. Their friends from the surrounding Gloucester countryside were known as the 'Glosse Posse' and were all children of wealthy locals.

His GCSE results were not made public, but the extent of his social life soon was.

CHAPTER EIGHT

Under the African sun

If the events of Harry's social life in 2001 were the bender, then the hangover came in January 2002, when it was reported that he had spent the previous summer under-age drinking and smoking marijuana. Harry was angry that he had been singled out for blame while William's reputation was left unblemished. It was reported that Charles made Harry go to a rehab centre to speak with addicts and learn about the effects of substance abuse, but in truth he had been there before the story was released in the paper, and the two events were unrelated.

He did have more watchful eyes on him, however, and as well as staying with family friends now any time that his father was away, he also channelled his energies into his love of the military. He threw himself into the Combined Cadet Force. The CCF is a Ministry of Defence sponsored youth organization, available to many schools across the country. Its aim is to encourage members to take responsibility and develop leadership skills, as well as self-reliance, resourcefulness and endurance through military-themed and adventurous activities. This was nothing like the one-off visits to military bases he'd come to enjoy as a young boy – the clambering into tanks and specially created children's fatigues were enough to whet his appetite, but now he was taking on weapons training, and learning battle skills, signals and shooting. In schools, the CCF is built into the timetable, exercises are undertaken on some weekends – including one involving live fire – and summer camp.

Harry's family was going through a tough time. Despite it being the Queen's Golden Jubilee year, there wasn't much personally for the Queen to celebrate, as in February her sister, Harry's great-aunt Princess Margaret, died in her sleep after complications following a stroke. They were a close-knit family and the Queen's only sibling had been a neighbour to Harry when he was growing up in Kensington Palace, so her death affected them all. Just six weeks later, the Queen Mother died in her sleep at the age of 101. Naturally the family felt the loss deeply. Charles, Harry and William had been skiing in Klosters with friends when they heard the news. Charles, always so close to his grandmother, was devastated. The party flew back immediately. As well as dealing with the personal side of their bereavement, the Queen Mother's death also meant changes within the royal household. Charles and the boys moved from York House into her former residency, Clarence House, which stands next to St James's Palace and had been built in 1828 for the Duke of Clarence, later William IV. It had been home to Princess Elizabeth and Prince Philip after they married, and they stayed there until Princess Elizabeth became Queen. The Queen Mother then moved in, remaining there until her death.

Several million pounds' worth of refurbishments were

undertaken, but, in tribute to his grandmother, Charles kept one of the parlours just as the Queen Mother had left it. It remains a traditional property, with a powder-blue morning room, garden room, and furnishings of gilt mirrors, marble fireplaces and gold leaf furniture. Harry and William had rooms there, which they used when they returned from school.

The Queen put on a brave face and celebrated her Golden Jubilee with her people in June. As his eighteenth birthday approached, Harry started taking on more royal duties and when he celebrated his birthday he was appointed his own coat of arms and standard. He was also becoming more involved with the charity sector, visiting homeless children, drug addicts in shelters, and, later, Great Ormond Street Hospital.

In September he attended the service of thanksgiving in commemoration of the 9/11 terrorist attacks of the previous year. Giving his first official press interview to commemorate his eighteenth birthday, where he spoke of Diana's work with AIDS charities and landmines, Harry added, 'She had more guts than anyone else. I want to carry on the things that she didn't quite finish. I have always wanted to, but was too young.'

He revealed that his father had offered him a party at home to commemorate his landmark birthday, but he turned it down and celebrated quietly with his family instead. However, he showed he'd kept his sense of humour, joking that he would have a four-year gap year.

He was photographed in his room at Eton and from the photographs a few details of his personal tastes could be pieced together. Alongside a poster for rock radio station XFM, was a St George's cross flag – he is very proud of his country, but his globetrotting also means that he has a passion for many other cultures too, which was demonstrated in the colourful memorabilia from his trips abroad on the walls around him, including a wall-hanging woven with elephants. As well as a busty blonde pinup and a bikini girl, he had also tacked up cut-outs of other models on top of the hanging, while a framed picture of his mother stood on his desk. Despite being third in line to the throne, like many young men around the country he appeared to favour Lynx deodorant.

It had been quite a year for the young prince, who was just coming of age. While most teenagers would have to deal with the wrath of their parents if they discovered they were drinking underage and using illegal drugs, teenaged Harry had to face any indiscretions being made public knowledge, commented on and dissected. Additionally, his great-aunt and great-grandmother had both passed away. However, nothing could have prepared him for the terrible news he received in December 2002, when his close friend, Henry van Straubenzee, died in a car crash.

Harry had known Henry since they were children. Diana had been friends with Henry's uncle Willie, and the two boys also went to Ludgrove School together, while William was good friends with Henry's older brother, Thomas. Harry and William had often been on holiday with the van Straubenzees to Rock in Cornwall.

Henry had returned to Ludgrove to teach, and was then about to spend six months teaching in Uganda before starting at Newcastle University. He had won an army scholarship, so the MoD was sponsoring his degree, after which he would have gone to Sandhurst.

On the night of his death, Henry and a friend were celebrating the end of term at a school party when the music system broke down, so the pair drove down the school driveway to borrow a CD player from another friend, and on their way back, Henry's friend lost control of the car and crashed into the only tree in the vicinity.

They had been on a private driveway, so neither was wearing seat belts and, as it was an old car, there was no airbag. Henry was killed instantly and his friend was badly injured. Later, Henry's mother Claire wrote formally to the police urging them not to prosecute Henry's friend, the driver, later explaining to the *Evening Standard*, 'Both of them were drunk. Either of them could have been driving. It doesn't matter.'

The funeral was held just before Christmas, and there was a thanksgiving service in January, where the substantial amount of money raised by the collection prompted Henry's parents to think about starting up a charity in their son's name. They travelled to Uganda to learn about what kind of work Henry would have been doing and then set up the Henry van Straubenzee Memorial Fund, which aims to improve the quality of education in Ugandan schools.

For Harry, the year ended with the funeral of one of his closest friends, and the next year began with his memorial service. He was back at Eton for his final year, but must have been affected by all that had happened.

*

In the spring of 2003 Harry had started dating Laura Gerard Leigh, a pretty eighteen-year-old daughter of a stockbroker. They had been introduced by Guy Pelly and she became part of Glosse Posse. Laura attended St Mary's School in Calne, and she would drive to watch Harry play the wall game at weekends, after which they would go for Sunday lunch in Windsor. Girls weren't allowed to be brought back to Manor House so the pair would frequently stay at Laura's parents' London home. The relationship fizzled out after four months, but they stayed friends. Before he left school, Harry took an opportunity to tread the boards when he played the villain's henchman Conrade in the Shakespeare comedy *Much Ado About Nothing*, and he did well in his final year art show, but it was still his passion for all things military that meant he excelled in the Combined Cadet Force. By the time he left, he had been promoted to Lance Corporal, and in the prestigious Annual Tattoo, he led a detachment of forty-eight cadets as they presented their colours to the 800 people present, among whom was Tiggy.

After dropping History of Art, Harry left Eton with a B in Art and a D in Geography. His results were not good enough for a university place but the army had always been his dream. 'I am very proud of Harry,' his father said in a public statement. 'He has worked hard for these examinations and I am very pleased with today's results.'

While Harry was pleased to be leaving school and continuing with the next stage of his life, there was someone else saying goodbye to Eton who wasn't so happy about it. The school had decided not to renew the contract of one of Harry's History of Art teachers, Sarah Forsyth, and she filed a lawsuit, claiming unfair dismissal. Later in court, she claimed that the head of Art Ian Burke undermined and bullied her, and that he had helped Harry cheat in his final exams. She claimed that the night before a moderator was due at the school, she was asked by Burke to prepare some text that should have been written by the prince to go with one of his artworks. A tribunal ruled that Forsyth was sacked unfairly, finding that Burke 'did undermine and bully her', but they rejected her claims that she had helped Harry cheat, and his name was cleared.

That summer Harry celebrated leaving school, partying under the watchful eye of Mark Dyer, who also helped to organize Harry's gap year. In September, Harry turned nineteen and flew to Tooloombilla, Queensland, Australia, to be a jackaroo – an Australian term for a cowboy – for two months. His duties included rounding up livestock in thick scrub, branding animals, and chores such as fencing. He stayed in a simple weatherboard cottage on a farm owned by Noel and Annie Hill. Noel Hill is the son of polo-player Sinclair Hill, who had coached Prince Charles, and Annie had been a friend of Diana's. Harry was paid the equivalent of £100 a week. Unfortunately, things didn't go according to plan and the paparazzi swarmed over the cattle station, even thicker than the black outback flies. It meant Harry couldn't work properly and, in a fit of pique, angrily declared he was going to go home. His press team were forced to issue a statement, 'He wants to learn about outback trades, not dodge the cameras.' In exchange for a photo call, he was eventually left to go about his work.

After Tooloombilla, he then moved on to Sydney, where he made a quick stop in Taronga Zoo for a photo call with a koala, and then supported the England rugby team who were over there for the World Cup, and went out drinking with his cousin Zara Philips and her boyfriend Mike Tindall, who was playing for England.

When his work was done Down Under, Harry returned home for a brief visit, and on a night out to London club Chinawhite he exchanged kisses and numbers with glamour model Lauren Pope, who went on to star in TV reality show *The Only Way is Essex*, although nothing else happened between them.

For the second part of his gap year, Prince Charles's new communications secretary, Patrick Harverson, accompanied

Harry to Africa, and it was a trip that would change Harry's life forever. Charles had selected Lesotho for Harry to visit because nearly half the population live below the poverty line, and it has one of the highest rates of AIDS in the world. Life expectancy is put at just forty-one years, and, staggeringly, around a quarter of the population are orphans, many of them HIV positive themselves. Harry was to be working with many of these children.

So, in February, Harry and his friend George Hill, accompanied by Patrick Harverson, flew to Lesotho, a tiny, lush, mountainous high-altitude country entirely land-locked in South Africa. The country is so small that sometimes it doesn't appear on maps, while many of the population live in highland villages that can only be reached by foot or on horseback. Harry shaved his head and arrived for his two-month stay on the back of a truck. He and his friend spent half an hour building a wire mesh around the orphanage compound and then Harry played with the children. He also helped build a fence and plant trees at the Mants'ase Children's Home in Mohales Hoek.

Harry took to the country and its people very quickly and soon struck up a friendship with the kingdom's Prince Seeiso. 'When we first met, Prince Harry was just a young man on his gap year,' says the prince. 'It was a pleasure to show him round Lesotho. While we grew up in very different countries, I think we have a lot in common and have a really close bond. We have similar values.'

Prince Seeiso could also see how good Harry was with the children he met, recalling, 'I remember the way in which Prince Harry instantly connected with the children and how friendly and relaxed he was with everyone. He has a real way with children and I think this is obvious to anyone who has seen the way he interacts with them. They really warm to him.'

Harry had also brought with him rugby balls and footballs so he could play with the children. In one emotional encounter he was close to tears when he held a ten-month-old girl named Liketsu who had been raped by a man infected with AIDS who had been told by a witch doctor that having sex with a child would cure him. Harry was very moved and secretly returned the following year to see how Liketsu was doing.

One of the biggest problems was – and still is – knowing exactly how many children are living with HIV. Another is lack of education. More children needed to be tested, and after any diagnosis they need to be educated to understand the importance of taking the drugs that can help them. Harry was interested in the herd boys, a vulnerable group of young boys who go to work with cattle in the mountains and do not come down into the villages very often.

As he left the tiny kingdom, and in the months that followed, he felt that he wanted to help the people as much as he could, and within a year his thoughts were put into action.

*

In April 2004 he flew on to Cape Town, where he experienced a second life-changing event on his African trip, when he met up with a girl he had first encountered back in the UK. At eighteen, she was a year younger than him and they had met through mutual friends when they were at school in the same area. She was blonde, curvy and pretty, with bee-stung lips and a broad smile that lit up her face, but Chelsy Yvonne Davy was more than just her looks. She was smart, fun and funny. She had also been born and raised in Harry's beloved Africa, and she could shoot, ride bareback, and kill a snake with her bare hands. No wonder he wanted to make the effort to see her again.

Chelsy was born in Zimbabwe on 13 October 1985 to Charles, a hunting safari operator, and Beverley, a former Miss Coca-Cola Rhodesia. Along with younger brother Shaun, she grew up surrounded by the vast, wild African bush as her family owned 1,300 acres in the Lemco Safari Area. In such remote and beautiful surroundings, sitting outside under a conical thatched roof in a garden surrounded by acacia trees has been described as having a 'fairy-tale' feel. Hunting in Africa is still big business., and although species such as the endangered black rhino are protected, Chelsy's father could charge up to £17,000 for the chance to shoot lion, elephant, leopard and buffalo on twenty-four-day expeditions.

Chelsy had been living in England since she was thirteen, when her parents enrolled her at Cheltenham College. She then moved on to Stowe school, which is where, through a mutual friend, she met Harry. Nothing happened between them at that stage because Chelsy knew she was going back to South Africa, where she had a place at Cape Town University to study politics, philosophy and economics.

By the time Harry caught up with her in 2004, she was in her first year at the university, however student digs weren't for her, and she lived with her brother in her parents' beachfront apartment in Camps Bay. She and Harry enjoyed spending time together during the remainder of Harry's trip, as they whipped up the coastline in her silver Mercedes and she showed him the sights of Cape Town. He also got to know her brother Shaun, which was important to her as, like Harry, she has a close-knit family.

By the time Harry flew back to the UK, he was hooked –

he loved Africa, and one part of it in particular. Even though it would be a twelve-hour flight any time he wanted to see Chelsy, it's one that Harry took many times in the next few years.

In June 2004, his maternal grandmother Frances Shand Kydd died, which deeply saddened both him and William. They still spent time with their mother's side of the family, and their grandmother had, of course, been another link to Diana. The princes attended her funeral and spent some time with their maternal relations.

Harry kept busy over the summer, playing polo with Charles and William at Cirencester Park Polo Club for the Gurkha Welfare Challenge Trophy, and completing a charity run alongside William and Gordon Ramsay for Sport Relief. In September he turned twenty and took the Regular Commissions Board (RCB) test to get into the Royal Military Academy Sandhurst.

Sandhurst is where all officers in the British Army are trained to take on the responsibilities of leading soldiers. It is a state-funded organization, and no one can pay to go there, but the selection process is tough. The extensive four-day RCB test was held in an old army barracks in Westbury, Wiltshire, and covered a wide range of skills including academic written exams, physical tests, verbal reasoning (which evaluates the ability to think constructively), and psychometric testing (which assesses psychological abilities). Potential recruits are graded on how they present their information. They are also split into groups and given tasks to see how they solve problems. On some occasions the group has a designated leader to see how that individual handles the pressure, and on other occasions there is no designated leader, to see who has natural leadership skills. A former officer cadet recalls, 'They look at how you interact with everyone else, and you also get interviewed to death – especially if you haven't been to university. It's an intense four days.'

Harry passed the test and, since Sandhurst takes on new recruits three times a year, this meant that he was all set to join in January 2005.

*

Harry was still learning to juggle his increasing royal responsibilities with his private life. Rather than blending the two, he saw them as different entities, and so when he felt he was on private time, he was frustrated, angry, sometimes emotional about the constant attention he received. He was twenty and like most others his age he was enjoying hitting the clubs and bars of London with his friends to drink, smoke, talk and dance. In October there was a scuffle with photographers outside London club Pangaea, during which he was held back by his protection officer. The paparazzo on the receiving end of Harry's anger suffered a cut lip, but didn't press charges. There was growing concern for the way Harry was conducting himself in public, and the fact that he was vulnerable as he left these high-profile nightspots.

The following month he left with his friends Mark and Luke Tomlinson for the final part of his gap year in Argentina, where he worked on the El Remanso polo estate in Buenos Aires for six weeks. While he was there, Chelsy visited him for a weekend and they flew by private jet to the Entre Ríos province in Mesopotamia. The lovebirds were also back in each other's arms just before Christmas, when they holidayed on the sandy island of Bazaruto off the coast of Mozambique, East Africa, with Chelsy's family.

During a traditional royal Christmas at Sandringham, the family were as stunned as the rest of the world to hear of the terrible Boxing Day tsunami in the Indian Ocean, when around 200,000 people were killed. Harry and William immediately wanted to do whatever they could to help, and worked with other volunteers in a Red Cross warehouse loading aid packages to be sent to those affected. They also made a sizeable donation to the relief fund from their own private money. After watching the devastation unfold, William said, 'We were watching a documentary about orphans. It brought tears to our eyes.' While Harry added, 'We just wanted to be hands on. We didn't want to sit back.' Harry later also became patron of a charity called MapAction, which provides essential mapping information to aid charities in the wake of natural and humanitarian disasters such as the tsunami.

Despite the fact that he was champing at the bit to begin his military career, Harry was unable to start at Sandhurst in January 2005 because of a knee injury he had sustained while teaching rugby to children the previous October. He had recently become involved with the Rugby Football Union's All Schools campaign, and visited a number of schools to help get more children involved with the game. So his start at Sandhurst was delayed until the spring.

While he wasn't physically fit enough for the punishing regime at Sandhurst, he could still go about his everyday life until he gave himself over to the rigours of his military training. He and William had been invited to their friend Harry Meade's birthday party and, as with many of their friends' parties, there was a fancy dress theme. For his twenty-first, William had chosen 'Out of Africa' and his new girlfriend Kate Middleton selected a 1920s theme for hers. Harry Meade had selected

'Native and Colonial'. It was, in simple terms, a broader version of 'Cowboys and Indians' but the theme was later criticized due to the nature of colonialism – those from one territory expanding into someone else's and therefore perhaps it was an insensitive theme for a group of wealthy Western kids.

CHAPTER NINE

Broken down and re-built

The theme of the party wouldn't even have been made public, were it not for Harry's choice of costume – and the fact that one of the guests took a picture of him wearing it and sold it to a newspaper. Partygoers wore safari suits, or cowboys and Indians outfits. William opted for a lion costume complete with black leggings and big paws, while their friend Guy Pelly played it for laughs and dressed as the Queen. Harry, meanwhile, opted for a Second World War Nazi uniform, which he had hired from Maud's Cotswold Costumes around the corner from Highgrove. He had looked at SS costumes, but because they were only available in small, he opted for the sand-coloured outfit because he thought it complemented his colouring. No one around him led him to question his choice of costume – from his protection officers, to those in his household – and if his brother did make any comments to him about his questionable choice, Harry certainly didn't pay any heed. A few days later a picture of him in his costume, with the swastika armband clearly on display, was splashed across the front page of the *Sun* after one of the guests sold the picture to the paper.

There would never have been a good time for Harry to be photographed in a Nazi uniform, but when it did happen, it couldn't have been at a much worse time. It was just days before the sixtieth anniversary of the liberation of Auschwitz, a ceremony that Prince Edward was due to attend as a mark of respect.

Through his press office, Harry immediately issued an apology, stating, 'I am very sorry if I caused any offence or embarrassment to anyone. It was a poor choice of costume and I apologize.' He still received a great deal of criticism from the media, because the apology seemed like nothing more than a platitude. There was speculation about whether or not he should be allowed to take up his place at Sandhurst, as the college had already stated that he would be treated like anyone else, and questions were raised as to whether another individual would be permitted to join if they had made a similar mistake.

Ken Wharfe believes that the lines of communication were not as strong as they should have been between Harry and his protection officers. 'In the past I don't think he has thought things through as well as he should have done,' says Wharfe. 'We all know Harry had no intention of insulting the Jewish community. It wouldn't have crossed his mind. For him it was a joke. What he wasn't thinking was "what might be the repercussions?" Someone needed to say to him, "Sir, do you think this is a good idea?" I would have said, "Harry, this is going to drop you in the s*** if you don't mind me saying, Sir."' Wharfe would have been correct, figuratively and literally, as under his father's instruction, Harry spent the rest of the month working at Charles's Duchy Home Farm, part of the Highgrove estate, where one of his chores was mucking out the pigs.

*

Harry and William were young adults now, and it was agreed that they could start setting up their own office, under the umbrella of their father's. Harry had recently made a very public mistake but the hope was that taking on more responsibilities would encourage him to become more responsible. William was approaching his twenty-third birthday and that year he would be finishing university, and both he and Harry were preparing for Sandhurst and their subsequent military careers, while also taking on more royal duties and charity work.

Former SAS officer Jamie Lowther-Pinkerton was appointed part-time private secretary to both princes. Lowther-Pinkerton had been equerry to the Queen Mother, before working as a professional soldier for twenty years, returning to royal service in 2005 with his appointment to the princes. He was to become a solid and trusted figure to both boys in their young adulthood. Meanwhile, Helen Asprey, a member of the famous jewellery family, had moved over from the Duke of Edinburgh's office at Buckingham Palace to become their personal private secretary. She organized their personal life – their doctor and dentist appointments, diarizing their appointments, their polo matches and shooting events, booking their flights for work, organizing their holidays and doing their shopping. She also accompanied the princes on some of their first public engagements.

Around this time the brothers' two girlfriends, Chelsy Davy and Kate Middleton, met for the first time when Chelsy flew over to see Harry play in a polo match. She and Harry had been together for a year by this time, and that year Harry had already been out to Botswana with Chelsy, where they went on safari. Kate had been with William for two years and asked Chelsy if she would like to go shopping with her in London, but Chelsy declined. The girls got on fine, but the English rose and the African wildflower were not a natural fit.

While his sons enjoyed their first flushes of young love, Prince Charles was preparing to marry the woman he had first fallen in love with some thirty years earlier. Before the big day, he took a small group skiing in Klosters as a sort of stag-do. Harry, William and Kate were part of that party, along with a couple of the brothers' friends. They went to Casa Antica, a long-time favourite with young guests at the resort, including the royals. The group was in high spirits and on one night tussled during a play-fight in which they were trying to determine whether Harry was going 'commando'. His beaded bracelet – a present from Chelsy – was torn off and he was to be found scrabbling around on the floor trying to pick the beads up.

They were all on best behaviour the following month, however, when Charles and Camilla exchanged their vows in Windsor Guildhall. The Queen did not attend, believing her role of Supreme Governor of the Church of England should not allow it as the couple were both divorcees, but she was there for the service of prayer and dedication in St George's Chapel at Windsor Castle afterwards, which was followed by an afternoon reception. Harry and William gave out a whoop when Charles and Camilla exchanged their vows. In the eight years since they had first been introduced to Camilla as their father's partner, William and Harry had gone from distrustful young boys with conflicting emotions, to forming a loving adult relationship with their new stepmother. Harry said, 'To be honest with you, she's always been very close to me and William … She's not the wicked stepmother. Everyone has to understand it's very hard for her. Look at the position she's coming into. Don't feel sorry for me and William, feel sorry for her. We're very happy to have her around.'

After an afternoon tea of smoked salmon sandwiches, cakes, tarts and fudge, Harry and Camilla's son Tom decorated the car and raced across the grass to be the last ones to see the honeymooners out of the gate.

Camilla had become a cherished member of the family, and is also a clear favourite with the royal press pack, thanks to her warm, unfussy and friendly manner, as well as her consummate professionalism. *Sunday Express* royal correspondent Camilla Tominey explains, 'The Duchess of Cornwall is great fun. What I like about her is that she doesn't really seem to have been changed by royal life. What you see is what you get – she's quintessentially English in a country mumsy way.' She continues, 'Of course she will forever be haunted by Princess Diana referring to her as the "third person" in her marriage to Charles but I think a lot of the ill feeling towards her has died down now. I think people now accept that she makes Charles happy, and in that respect she is going to be instrumental in making him a better King.'

Meanwhile, award-winning photographer Chris Jackson, who works for top picture agency Getty Images, has been travelling the world photographing the Duchess for over ten years. He adds, 'You will quite often find yourself among some weird and wonderful people in various corners of the world, and Camilla will always flash you that knowing smile, occasionally stifling giggles during some of the more amusing situations you come across. During a dance performance from some Tanzanian teenagers while we were on a tour of Eastern and Southern Africa, some of the language became quite "choice" as they emulated some of their favourite rappers, but the Duchess managed to maintain her decorum while the media were listening in shock at some of the "lyrics". Flashing the occasional knowing smile at the media, we can only guess what she was thinking!'

*

In May 2005, Harry finally realized the next stage of his army dreams when he enrolled at Sandhurst. One of the roles of the royal family is to serve their country, and so all of the men in the family have been through military training so that they can do just this. Traditionally, the Windsors always served in the navy, including the Duke of Edinburgh, Prince Charles and Prince Andrew. However, Harry had always had a passion for the army. He arrived knowing that he had a challenging forty-eight weeks ahead of him, including the especially gruelling first five weeks.

The Royal Military Academy Sandhurst in Surrey was formed in 1947 from two pre-existing training colleges and has trained officers from all over the world as well as famous Brits Sir Winston Churchill, actor David Niven and singer James Blunt. The purpose of Sandhurst training is to break down unhelpful habits so that the cadets can be remoulded, in order to be capable of enduring the rigours of war, while leading a troop of men. Meanwhile, the army's primary task is to help defend the interests of the UK, and this may involve service overseas or being deployed on UN operations, and used to help in other emergencies. At the end of the course a newly commissioned officer will be qualified to lead and manage soldiers while at the same time upholding the British Army's core values of selfless commitment, respect for others, loyalty, integrity, discipline and courage. The training at Sandhurst covers weapons training, signalling, patrolling and military law, with lectures on numerous other areas including communications and interpersonal relationships, plus physical exercise and role-play. Each newly enrolled Officer Cadet then goes out on exercise to put into practice what they have learned. They all also receive media training where Officer Cadets are filmed in order to study how they act, what they say and how they say it.

On 8 May 2005, Harry, accompanied by Prince Charles, made the journey up the long, straight drive flanked by immaculate lawns to the nineteenth-century Old School building, a distinctive long two-storey cream building with a classical-style entrance. Each intake of Officer Cadets tends to have particular characteristics, and as a Sandhurst alumni explains, 'September tends to be school leavers and university graduates who know they've been going into the army for a long time, and they are nicknamed "thrusters"; in January they tend to be more down to earth – people who've taken time off and chilled and who are not so "army", and then in May you tend to get the bohemians thinking, "Army? Why not?"' Harry had been wanting to join the army since he was old enough to speak, but he was enrolling alongside an eclectic bunch.

Six weeks before starting he had been given a list of all the things he needed to bring with him and was fully equipped with, among other items, his boot-cleaning kit, a specific number of coat hangers, padlocks and an iron and ironing board. He was now Officer Cadet Wales for the year-long duration of the training. The Sandhurst alumni continues, 'The best way to imagine Sandhurst is like everyone's first day of school. I remember the smell from that first day; it's an old smell – floor polish and Brasso and antique wood. Everyone's in their chinos and jacket and looking very smart. Nervous with it. You're looking around for familiar faces from the RCB. You're all shoehorned into a room and the instructors tell your parents, "I will be looking after your son for the next however many months". It's very much like they're saying "I will be your son's Latin teacher". Then the parents leave, the door shuts behind them and everything changes.'

Within ten minutes, everyone has a badge with their surname prefixed by 'Officer Cadet' on it. Everything happens at such speed on that first day, and there are so many briefings and so much administration, that it can often be 2 a.m. before the new recruits find themselves in their rooms in bed. For the first five weeks, new recruits are not allowed to leave the grounds, they are only allowed in certain areas, so that they can bond with their platoon. There are no laptops or phones allowed, no alcohol, no TV and all radios are tuned to BBC Radio 4. The men's heads are also shaved. They are up before dawn and immediately prepare for inspection – their uniform has to be crisply pressed, boots polished, beds made with hospital corners, and belongings in their room set up uniformly with exact spaces in between, all by 5.30 a.m. If mistakes were made there would be press-ups for the whole platoon. They reported for duty every day, and on Sundays there was chapel.

The Officer Cadets were kept busy from the moment they were on their feet to the minute they went to bed. Even sitting down for lunch they would have to eat fast and not let going to the loo or cleaning their weapons take up too much time, because whenever the bell rang they would have to be up again – whether they had finished eating or not. They were answerable to their Colour Sergeant – their immediate point of contact. Smart, immaculate and fearsome, the colour sergeant would teach them everything they needed to know. As the new recruits are learning to be the best of the best, it is assumed that they know nothing, so they are even taught how to wash and shave themselves properly. The Sandhurst alumni explains, 'The Colour Sergeant is who you wanted to be. You get brainwashed into thinking "I want to look like that, I want to be as smart as that". They were never happy, nothing was ever good enough and they were always angry. They were on you constantly – whenever you think you can relax, they will reappear.' Harry's Colour Sergeant was Glenn Snazle from the Grenadier Guards.

Officer Cadets have to march everywhere, calling out the timing until they are good enough not to (the Colour Sergeant will decide when that is). The alumni explains, 'When you walk into an office, you'll call out "Halt. Check. One. Two" and then when you stand to attention, as you're slamming your foot down, you'll say "punch". It's an amusing time because there are some people who don't get the timing. It's just walking but because it's exaggerated people tend to over-think it by putting forward the wrong arm with wrong leg, which is called tick-tocking. It's really funny to watch men tick-tocking along all wrong. Grown men who can't walk properly.' Everyone has to march in pairs at all times, so even if an Officer Cadet wanted to go to the on-site Spar shop, they would have to find someone to go with them, and if there was a group of three who fancied going, they would need to find a fourth to make up two pairs.

The cadets went on several exercises each term in order to practise what they had learned. Most of them were held in the South-West. The first exercise is called 'self-reliance' and served to put into practice basic skills that have been learned, but is nicknamed 'self-abuse' as in those early days no one really knows what they're doing. It is usually cold, wet and tough for everyone.

Harry thrived at Sandhurst – he hadn't been very academic at school, but this suited him better. He did a six-hour race across the Black Mountains in the Brecon Beacons in record time, and scored top marks in one training exercise. In the final term they headed to Cyprus – where there are still British troops based – for a hot weather exercise.

Chelsy was still studying at Cape Town University, but once Harry's first five weeks were over, she flew over to be with him as often as possible during his weekend breaks. After the first five weeks the Officer Cadets could also use the bars at Sandhurst, although most didn't usually drink much because of the early starts and the physically demanding days. However, in September, Harry celebrated his twenty-first birthday with a few drinks in the Sandhurst bar. Unlike his friends, whose families splashed out on lavish costume parties, after the events earlier in the year he played it safe and celebrated with his fellow Officer Cadets in the basic confines of the bar.

However, he had already taken Chelsy and some of his friends on holiday to the Okavango Delta in Botswana, where he had first visited as a young teenager. There, the rains in the Angolan Highlands surge down the river to create a marshy water world of lagoons and rivers teeming with fish, birds and animals. They had sailed down the Okavango River on an old restored wooden houseboat called Kubu Queen, sleeping in a tent on the roof at night, and drifting along the water in the day. Extra crates of beer were delivered to the party, and Harry also went fishing.

Officially, his landmark birthday was marked with his first television interview, where he came across as more gentle than his party prince reputation, as well as more forthright and informal than his father and brother. He said his father was 'much more relaxed' since he had married Camilla, adding:

'She's a wonderful woman and she's made our father very, very happy, which is the most important thing. William and I love her to bits and get on really well with her.'

He spoke about his relationship with William, 'Every year we get closer, and we've even resorted to hugging each other now after not seeing each other for long periods of time. He is the one person on this earth that I can actually talk to about anything and we understand each other.' However, he wouldn't be drawn on his relationship with Chelsy, explaining: 'I'd love to tell everyone how amazing she is but once I start talking about that then I leave myself open in the future and if anyone asks me in the future they will say "you told them, why aren't you telling us?"'

He spoke about his desire to go to the front line explaining, 'I wouldn't have joined the army unless I was going to. If they said I couldn't then there's no way I would drag my sorry ass through Sandhurst.' And he also spoke about his choice of fancy dress outfit earlier in the year, 'Looking back on it now … It was a very stupid thing to do and I've learned my lesson.' William, who had just finished university, was set to start at Sandhurst. At that time Harry joked, 'When I have left, I'll have to make a special effort to visit him for comedy value, just so he can salute me.'

To coincide with his birthday, Harry was also made a Counsellor of State, which means that along with Princes Philip, Charles, William and Andrew, he can stand in for the Queen at Privy Council meetings and carry out some of her official duties in her absence.

After the annual Christmas celebrations at Sandringham, in January William joined Harry at Sandhurst, and, later that month, their father's office announced that Harry was to join the Household Cavalry (Blues and Royals) when he left the academy. The various regiments of the British Army would send representatives to Sandhurst each year for a kind of recruitment fair, where they would encourage the best Officer Cadets to join their regiment, while the Officer Cadets would explore the different regiments to decide which would be the best for them. The Household Cavalry was an obvious choice for Harry because it is one of the Queen's regiments – very traditional and highly respected. Harry had been at Sandhurst for eight months and it suited him. His energy and passion finally had a direction.

The Sovereign's Parade at the end of each term marks the passing out of the freshly minted Officers. During the ceremony, awards are given by the Sovereign's representatives to the top Officer Cadets. On 12 April 2006, when Harry and his fellow Officers passed out, the Queen herself took the salute. She was accompanied by the Duke of Edinburgh, while the Prince of Wales and new Duchess of Cornwall also attended, as did William as an Officer Cadet. It was the first time Harry had formally achieved something of significance before William and he milked it, laughing that William would have to salute him on the day. Tiggy, Mark Dyer and Jamie Lowther-Pinkerton were also there for his big day, although Chelsy stayed away from the formal event, and just attended in the evening.

The Queen addressed the cadets and wished them luck in their future careers, and then, according to tradition, Major Stephen Segrave rode his horse up the steps of Old College as Harry and his platoon slow-marched into the building, accompanied by the band trumpeting 'Auld Lang Syne'.

After a formal lunch with friends, family and regimental Officers, the day concluded in spectacular style with the commissioning ball. The Sandhurst gymnasium had been decorated with white flowers and scented candles, and there was a jazz band, a casino, a vodka luge and chocolate fountains.

When Harry saw Chelsy there in a clingy backless turquoise silk dress with a deep tan, it was the first time he had seen her since their New Year holiday, and they made up for lost time, sharing cigarettes, champagne and kisses. At midnight there was the traditional fireworks display, spelling out 'congratulations', while all of the newly commissioned Officers tore the patches off the sleeves of their uniforms to reveal their Officer's pips. Harry was now a second lieutenant in the Household Cavalry, and within weeks would be training with his regiment and preparing for war.

CHAPTER TEN

'Forget-me-not'

Harry returned to Africa in April 2006 to follow in his mother's footsteps. One of the things closest to Diana's heart was her work with those who were affected by HIV, and when Harry had said during the interview to mark his eighteenth birthday that he wanted to continue his mother's work, they weren't just empty words.

When he had visited the mountain kingdom of Lesotho the previous year, he had been accompanied by ITN political correspondent Tom Bradbury, and a documentary – *The Forgotten Kingdom* – was made, which was shown on ITV. An appeal was launched off the back of the documentary, and the funds raised were used to set up a new charity, Sentebale, which was founded by Harry and Lesotho's Prince Seeiso.

'I want to carry on my mother's legacy as much as I can,' explained Harry. 'I don't want to take over from her because I never will ... But I want to carry on her work ... For most people it's been a long time since she died – but not for me.'

Prince Seeiso is also the second son of his country's royal family, and he had also lost his mother. Sadly, he had also lost his father. He explains, 'When I was younger, during the school holidays, I would go on horseback to my father's cattle posts and tend to his cattle, sheep, goats and horses. When Prince Harry visited in 2004 I took him to stay overnight in the mountains at one of our cattle posts and from here, the dream of Sentebale was born. Sentebale is a way in which both Prince Harry and I can honour the memory of our mothers, who both worked with vulnerable children, so it has a very special meaning for us.'

Meanwhile, Harry added, 'I'm not going to be some person in the royal family who just finds a lame excuse to go abroad and do all sorts of sunny holidays. I've always been like this, this is my side that no one gets to see. I believe I've got a lot of my mother in me, basically, and I just think she would want us to do this, me and my brother. Obviously, it's not as easy for William as it is for me. I think I've got more time on my hands to be able to help. I always wanted to go to an AIDS country to carry on my mother's legacy.'

The charity was set up to offer long-term support to community organizations working with young people, and in particular those working with orphans. The name Sentebale was chosen as it is a word that people in Lesotho use when they say goodbye to each other, and means 'forget-me-not'. The two princes thought it was perfect because they see Sentebale's work as a memorial to their mother's charity work, and its aim is to ensure that Lesotho and its children are not forgotten.

*

William and Harry were blazing their way into royal life,

and that spring they also set up the Princes' Charities Forum (later, when they were joined by the Duchess of Cambridge, the Charities Forum). William had already started taking on charity patronages, and Harry was about to, and it was William's idea to bring together representatives of all the charities they were working with for a twice-yearly meeting. The thought was that instead of the princes and their causes pulling in various different directions, it would benefit everyone if they could work together wherever possible, and it was the first time members of the royal family had worked together like this.

With 'Royal Harry' taken care of, it was time for 'Army Harry', and in May he began a twelve-week training programme at the Household Cavalry's headquarters at Bovington Camp in Dorset, where he would learn about working with tanks. He was now a second lieutenant and was beginning his Troop Leaders course, his training to become an armoured reconnaissance troop leader.

His weekends were free now, so there was also plenty of time for 'Off-duty Harry' and he would head back to London to party at the most exclusive bars and clubs. Boujis in Kensington was a particular favourite with him and his friends, as well as William and Kate. Sleek and sophisticated, the elite nightspot was lit purple and the ceiling was studded with miniature bulbs. The royal party was always whisked to the VIP room where they had their own barman. Harry and his friends would down Belvedere vodka mixed with Red Bull, and magnums of Dom Perignon champagne. The royal party would also drink rounds of Crack Baby cocktails – vodka and passion fruit juice topped with champagne and served in a test tube. All bar bills were waived in a practice called 'the royal comp', as they were there so often they brought immeasurable publicity to the club.

In the neighbouring and equally well-heeled Chelsea, Harry frequented Raffles on the King's Road, a members-only nightclub where potential members have to be vetted by a panel of four, and successful applicants receive a Links of London membership card. Also on the King's Road was the less fancy new bar Public, which had been set up by Harry's friend Guy Pelly. It wasn't perhaps as high-end as some of their other watering holes, with a riveted bar, pillars and fairy lights, but Public operated a guest list, and so was still an exclusive spot. Harry also favoured Whisky Mist, a bar just off Park Lane in Mayfair that featured dark leather booths and low lighting. Just around the corner was another royal favourite, Mahiki, a club with a tropical theme. Its wicker chairs and exotic flower prints, with orange and yellow lighting, created that 'club tropicana' feel, and the signature £100 Treasure Chest cocktail, which serves eight and is made up of brandy and peach liqueur shaken with lime and sugar and topped with a bottle of Moët & Chandon champagne. Entry to the club was free before 9 p.m. – for those who could afford to stay there for more than a couple of drinks – and £15 after that.

After closing time, Harry and his friends often pushed on through till dawn at private parties, including at his friend Mark Dyer's house. The army officer turned publican let Harry and his friends use his basement flat as a hangout while police protection officers waited outside until Harry was ready to call it a night (or morning). The bright lights, big city whirl of neon and liquor, pounding music, flirty girls and lifted velvet ropes was a seductive siren song for the young prince in his early twenties, and inevitably he found himself in some boozy scrapes. On one occasion at a house party in Fulham he kissed an older mother of two, Catherine Davies, who later went on to marry and appear in the US reality show *The Real Housewives of*

DC as Catherine Ommanney.

Chelsy was understandably upset when this and other similar stories appeared in the papers. Geography made their relationship difficult – they were 6,000 miles apart, after all – and Harry was just twenty-one, and Chelsy was still only twenty. They were passionately in love, but they were also very young. They managed to sort out their differences, however, and spent the summer together in the UK. They rented a four-bedroom house fifteen minutes from his officer's mess, and in their free time they hung out with friends and partied in their favourite clubs.

In August 2006, former *News of the World* royal correspondent Clive Goodman was arrested for intercepting calls involving members of the royal household. Always sensitive to the machinations of the press, Harry and William had long held suspicions that their phone messages were being listened to and had raised the alarm. William had once left a joke message on Harry's voicemail, pretending to be Chelsy giving him a earbashing about going to a lap-dancing club, and it ended up in *News of the World*: this was just one of many examples of a seemingly inconsequential snippet of information ending up in a newspaper. They had also noticed that the voicemails on their mobile phones would register that they had already been listened to when they knew they hadn't. Because many of the messages were concerned with the logistics of flights and the princes' movements, the anti-terrorism squad became involved, and discovered not only that the messages were being hacked, but also by whom. Harry and William were, understandably, furious and decided to prosecute.

*

Harry arrived at his new barracks in Windsor in September 2006, and was once again faced with meeting a lot of new people who would all have their pre-existing opinions of him based on his public image. One of these new faces was soldier James Wharton. 'We didn't know what to expect,' recalls James. 'But we just found a soldier in uniform, ready to go.' James soon found it was the ordinary soldiers who treated Harry like a regular guy, while it was often Harry's fellow officers who were more star-struck by him. 'There would always be one or two officers sort of following him around because of who he was,' James remembers. 'It was usually the other officers who made more of a fuss about him, saying, "Oh you must come and meet such and such", and the rest of us would just raise an eyebrow. He would always know when people were treating him a certain way because of who he is. He's not a fool.'

Harry soon became a popular figure among the men – although as an officer he held a position of authority, he broke down barriers between himself and the soldiers under him by spending their mutual down-time chatting and asking about their lives – as well as sometimes sitting down with them to play computer games in their quarters. 'It wasn't usual behaviour for an officer to be checking up on the lads, making sure they were all right, asking which their favourite Xbox game is,' recalls James. 'I found him to be very much ahead of the curve in that way.' On seeing pictures of James with his ex-boyfriend, Harry commented that they looked good together, asking about his relationship, and about when he realized he was gay. 'He's a very good guy, and he's a good leader,' recalls James. 'He took the time to be interested in people, and he would remember what you told him. For example, in the eighteen months between me first working with him in Windsor, and the second time in Canada, he remembered everything about me. I was silently impressed by that. He asked, "Are you still with that guy?"'

'I was really blown away by the way he almost strips himself of his royal position when he puts his army uniform on,' says James. 'He becomes – even more than he should really – one of the lads. I mean, it's usually the officers, and then the lads. But on many occasions I felt that he had just slightly verged over that line and been one of the boys for a couple of hours, by sitting around with us, talking and playing Xbox.' However, his attitude made him extremely popular with the men. 'The boys adored him,' reveals James. 'They listened to him and would do anything he told them to do, and I think it's because he is slightly left-field in his whole approach.'

In comparison, some of the officers didn't know how to speak to the ordinary man. 'Some officers come from the most privileged backgrounds,' explains James. 'For example, one of them is the great-great-great-great grandson of the Duke of Wellington, and I don't think he knows what it is to walk to a post office to post a letter, or pay a bill, and he talks incredibly posh. The boys were terrified of him, they just thought "this guy's an alien". Then Harry turns up and at the time he was third in line to the throne – you can't get more aristocratic than that – but he was the most down to earth.'

However, James's experience with Harry's brother William was slightly different. 'I feel like William is already King,' states James. 'We were all running in the park one day and I fell behind. I ended up with another squadron and realized I was running next to William. Because I knew I could joke with Harry, I stupidly thought I could be the same with William. So I said, "This is f***ing s***!" and the look he gave me was horrified. I thought, "Oh my God, what have I done?" That's when I realized how different they were. I dropped back a bit further after that!'

In October Harry flew to Cape Town for Chelsy's twenty-first birthday. She had a big party with a 'roaring twenties' theme and Harry got into the spirit by wearing a black-and-white pinstriped suit with braces and a white fedora. Underneath was a T-shirt that read, 'Spike Official Bodyguard of Miss CD'. Spike was a private nickname – he had a Facebook account under the name Spike Wells for four years on which he would leave messages for Chelsy or 'Chedda' as he called her. The following month, Chelsy graduated from the University of Cape Town with a degree in economics, and as she had gone straight from school to university, she took her gap year afterwards, spending much of the following year travelling with her brother Shaun.

Back in the UK, at the end of October the troops were sent on an exercise together in South Wales. Soldier James Wharton says that these exercises are often more physically strenuous than actually being away at war because there are constant tasks and tests to be completed, whereas at war the troops sleep more because they need to be fresh. However, during the arduous training, the men did enjoy the odd night out, and Harry, to their surprise, joined them when they went to the only nightclub in the whole area. 'It's an unwritten rule that the guys training out there go to this one horrendous nightclub, where you wouldn't ordinarily dream of going,' explains James. 'It was a horrible little place, the kind of place where you stick to the floor, and we all went out and got very, very drunk.'

However, it seems that even after a few drinks Harry was aware of the fact that he was an officer out with his men. 'I've never seen him in a drunken state,' says James. 'The next day we were all dreadful with hangovers, but I don't recall ever seeing him like that. I think he always keeps twenty per cent of his brain switched on when he's with his men – a little bit that just reminds him of who he is.' He was also very adept at misleading people as to who he is. 'One girl came over and said "Oh my God! You look just like Prince Harry,"' recalls James. 'And he said, cool as a cucumber, "I get that all the time" and the girl just walked off. Somehow he'd become camouflaged in his own skin.'

On the way back from Wales, Harry also managed to avoid being recognized because of his unlikely surroundings. 'We stopped at a service station on the M4 and we all queued up to get a Burger King,' remembers James. 'We were all in our uniform. Harry was in front of me, and behind me were two little old ladies and I heard one say to the other, "Do you know what, that's Prince Harry!" and the other one was going, "No, don't be ridiculous!" And they ended up having a row about whether it was him or not. When Harry got to the window, he didn't have any cash with him so someone had to buy his burger for him! Which I thought was amusing – I think he was reminded of that later.'

*

In December Harry and William announced they were going to organize a memorial concert for their mother to commemorate the tenth anniversary of her death. Around the same time the official and lengthy investigation into Diana's death was also concluded. Prince Charles, Prince Philip, the heads of MI5 and MI6 were among the four hundred people interviewed during the investigation. The verdict was that Diana died in a 'tragic accident', and that: 'There was no conspiracy to murder any of the occupants of the car'. The evidence suggested that Diana was not engaged or about to get engaged and tests showed that she was not pregnant, answering one rumour that was circulating. Prince Charles's press office put out a statement saying his sons hoped that the 'conclusive findings of the report would end speculation surrounding their mother's death'. But it was not to be. Mohamed Al Fayed remained convinced there had been foul play and so the case ground on.

In February 2007, at the age of twenty-two, Harry received news that he was to be sent on a tour of duty in Iraq that spring. It would be the first time a senior royal was going to the front line since Prince Andrew fought in the Falklands War twenty-five years earlier. The Queen is the only female member of the royal family who has served – during the Second World War she was an officer in the Auxiliary Territorial Service.

With that prospect in the near future, Harry turned his attention to royal duties, and took on his first royal patronage. Patronages are one of the key areas of importance for each member of the royal family. Over the years, they support a huge number of assorted projects and initiatives where they are able to help raise both funds and awareness by being associated with the charity. However, when a member of the royal family becomes a patron of a charity, the connection runs much deeper, and each charity is usually selected because it is very close to their heart for one reason or another.

Again, Harry showed how deeply he felt about the plight of the people of Lesotho and his fledgling charity Sentebale when he chose a little-known charity called Dolen Cymru to be the beneficiaries of his first patronage. The organization promotes friendship and understanding between the people of Wales and its twinned nation of Lesotho. In March, he also became patron of MapAction, after learning of its work when he helped out after the Asian tsunami, and WellChild, a charity that provides support for sick children and their carers across the UK.

Although he had been preparing mentally and physically for war, along with his troop of men, on 16 May it was announced that Harry would not be going to Iraq after all. Just weeks before, two men from the Queen's Royal Lancers had been killed out on an exercise that would have been part of Harry's deployment. Additionally, head of the army Sir Richard Dannatt explained, 'There has been a number of specific threats – some reported and some not reported – which relate directly to Prince Harry as an individual.' Those that had been reported were alarming enough – plots to kidnap him and smuggle him over the border into Iran; threats that he would be tortured and disfigured – so the fact that there were further threats was, naturally, a cause for concern.

Harry had grown up in William's shadow, emerging from early childhood shyness, struggling with dyslexia, and being held back at school. In his military career, he had found something he was very good at and felt he had come into his own – it's how he defines himself – so to find this out plunged him into a depression. James Wharton had trained with Harry and his troop so they were ready for their deployment, and he went out to Iraq when Harry did not. 'It was a nightmare,' remembers James. 'He did every single bit of training – and that training is hard – and we all got on the plane and went and he didn't. They had to keep his troop back in the UK for two weeks, and they couldn't be more than four hours from camp during that time in case a decision was made and they needed to go straight away. In the end they promoted a sergeant up one level to Staff Corporal Major, which gave him more responsibility, and he then became the troop leader. All the men knew him, and that was important, but they had to find a new sergeant from somewhere.'

Wharton says that even when he trained with Harry again a year later, it was still rankling that he hadn't been able to deploy with his men, recalling: 'He would say, "When I was meant to be in Iraq," and then pull a face that left no doubt he was still p***ed off about that.'

The Ministry of Defence sent Harry to Canada to be retrained as a battlefield air controller, which moving forward afforded his best chance of getting to the front line in the future. He was based in the British Army Training Unit in Suffield, 160 miles from Calgary, to spend three months learning how to carry out live-fire exercises in the vast expanse of prairie there.

He returned to London for the Diana Memorial Concert on 1 July 2007, which would have been his mother's forty-sixth birthday. Harry and William wanted it to be an upbeat, positive celebration of her life, and it benefited the princes' two charities, Centrepoint and Sentebale, and the five charities of which Diana was a patron when she died. The concert was held in the new Wembley Stadium and they made sure that the acts booked included Diana's favourite band Duran Duran, along with Take That, Lily Allen, Pharrell and Kanye West, as well as old favourites Tom Jones, Bryan Ferry and Rod Stewart. There was also a tribute to Diana's love of dance and theatre with a segment of 'Swan Lake' performed by the English National Ballet, and a medley of songs from Andrew Lloyd Webber musicals. 'We want it to represent exactly what our mother would have wanted,' William explained. 'We want to have this big concert on her birthday, full of energy, full of the sort of fun and happiness which I know she would have wanted. It's got to be the best birthday present she ever had.'

The concert was opened by Sir Elton John performing 'Your Song' against a backdrop of iconic black-and-white portraits of Diana by photographer Mario Testino. Elton John then introduced the princes, and the poignant note was clear, as the last time they and Elton were seen together in public was at Diana's funeral. Harry and William stood in front of a huge screen illuminated by a giant D, and to the 63,000 people Harry shouted, 'Hello Wembley!' as the crowd roared. This was an event for the younger members of the family and guests included Beatrice and Eugenie, Peter and Zara Phillips, Chelsy Davy and Kate Middleton, who had recently reunited with William after their short breakup, although they were taking it slowly and she sat a few rows back with her brother. William danced, Harry made fun of him. Chelsy was by his side.

To promote the concert, Harry and William gave an interview with the American TV channel NBC, where they admitted they never stopped wondering about how exactly Diana died, but dismissed conspiracy theories as nonsense. Harry said, 'For me personally, whatever happened … that night, in that tunnel … no one will ever know … I'll never stop wondering about that.' He also spoke about the fact that because of the length of the trial and the constant news coverage, it had been harder for him and William to come to terms with, adding: 'When you're being reminded about it, [it] does take a lot longer and it's a lot slower.' He also revealed that he would like to be a safari guide in South Africa.

Two months later, on 31 August, the memorial service marking the tenth anniversary of Diana's death was held at the Guards' Chapel at Wellington Barracks in London. It was attended by 500 friends, family, former employees and representatives from Diana's charities, and representing the Al Fayed family was the princes' former playmate from the summer of 1997, Dodi's half-sister Camilla. Complications arose around the invitation of Prince Charles's new wife Camilla, Duchess of Cornwall. However, William and Harry had invited her, and Charles wanted her to be there, but Camilla herself wasn't sure since many of the public still blamed her for Charles and Diana's break-up. Opinions voiced in the newspapers against her attending served to fan the flames. In the end, the Queen intervened and gave her blessing for Camilla to stay away. Camilla then issued a statement: 'On reflection, I believe my attendance could divert attention from the purpose of the occasion, which is to focus on the life and service of Diana.'

However, even though one potential problem had been averted, there were further issues to tackle between the families of Charles and Diana.

A friend of the family told Penny Junor for her book *Prince William: Born to be King*, 'William's quite complicated and Harry is not at all complicated. He's one of the most straightforward people I have ever met.' William was becoming exasperated by the inter-family politics of the seating plan in the chapel, and his press office went back and forth with Prince Charles trying to sort it out – it was getting complicated. In the end, Harry took it into his own hands, 'He just said "f*** that", picked up the phone and said "I want to speak to my father, put him through" and he just said, "Right, Dad, you're sitting here, someone else is sitting there and the reason we've done it is blah and blah. All right? Are you happy?" "Oh, yes," said Charles, "I suppose so."'

Inside the chapel, William sat next to the Queen on the front row and gave a reading from St Paul's letter to the Ephesians. Harry sat with the Spencers and paid a moving tribute to his mother. He began: 'William and I can separate our lives into two parts. There were those years where we were blessed by the physical presence beside us of both our mother and father. And then there are the ten years since our mother's death.' He went on to pay a simple, eloquent and moving tribute, 'When she was alive we took for granted her unrivalled love of life, laughter, fun and folly. She was our guardian friend and protector. She never once allowed her unfaltering love for us to go unspoken or undemonstrated … She was quite simply the best mother in the world. We would say that, wouldn't we? But we miss her. She kissed us last thing at night. Her beaming smile greeted us from school. She would laugh hysterically and uncontrollably when she remembered something silly she might have said or done that day.'

He finished by speaking poignantly of their loss, as well as expressing their hopes for the future: 'To lose a parent so suddenly at such a young age, as others have experienced, is indescribably shocking and sad. It was an event that changed our lives forever, as it must have done for anyone who lost someone that night. What is far more important to us now, and into the future, is that we remember my mother as she would wish to be remembered. As she was – fun-loving, generous, down to earth and entirely genuine. We both think of her every day, we speak about her and laugh together at all the memories. Put simply, she made us and so many other people happy. May this be the way she is remembered.'

Her favourite hymn 'I Vow to Thee My Country', which was played at her wedding and at her funeral, was also played at the memorial. And there were more flowers – they flowed through the Pont de l'Alma tunnel in Paris, and were massed once more at Kensington Palace and at her childhood home of Althorp.

As Harry turned twenty-three in September, Chelsy moved to the UK and started her postgraduate degree in law at Leeds University. He was late to the airport to pick her up, leaving her waiting for an hour. In October he missed her birthday and instead went to Paris to watch England play South Africa in a rugby match followed by a drinking session. He was still flirting with other girls. Chelsy was livid. She was also homesick in Leeds, living in a shabby part of town when she had been living in a glass-fronted apartment overlooking the beach in Cape Town. They were each other's first loves, however, so they talked through their issues and patched up their differences. Although Harry was about to be stationed to Afghanistan ...

CHAPTER ELEVEN

The reality of war

After Al-Qaeda's 9/11 terrorist attacks in the United States, the armed forces of the United States, United Kingdom, Australia, France and the Afghan United Front launched Operation Enduring Freedom, and the overseas forces sent their troops into Afghanistan. Their aim was to dismantle the global militant Islamist organization Al-Qaeda, founded and led by Osama Bin Laden. The leader was using Afghanistan as his base and had founded several terrorist training camps there. He had close connections to the Taliban, who were currently in power in Afghanistan. By the time Harry was deployed to Afghanistan, the Taliban government had been overthrown and the capital, Kabul, had been secured, but not much progress had been made into the countryside into which the Taliban had fled.

After his aborted mission to Iraq, this time it was decided that Harry would be flying out in secret, and only his family, senior MoD officials and the Prime Minister, Gordon Brown, knew he was going. Shortly before he flew out, members of the press were also informed – it was deemed better to make them aware of the highly sensitive nature of the mission because if Harry's cover was blown he would have to return, so the MoD wanted to minimize that risk. In return for the press agreeing not to report on Harry's deployment, they were promised an interview with him while he was stationed there, which would be conducted by a journalist from the UK news agency the Press Association, while a Press Association photographer would be permitted to fly out to capture images of Harry in the field.

In December 2007 Harry finally got to go to the front line. As Commander-in-Chief of the armed forces, the Queen was the person who informed him he was off to war, and Harry later said, 'She was very pro my going then, so I think she's relieved that I get the chance to do what I want to do. She's a very good person to talk to about it. Her knowledge of the army is amazing for a grandmother – I suppose it's slightly her job.'

He was to be forward air controller, based on the ground, controlling the air space and guiding jets with bombs, surveillance planes, troop transports and supply drops. He would also be responsible for scrutinizing hours of surveillance footage beamed from aircraft flying over enemy positions to a laptop terminal which became known as Taliban TV.

On 14 December 2007, dressed in desert fatigues, Harry boarded the military aircraft at RAF Brize Norton. As they entered Afghan airspace the troops put on their personal body armour and helmets, and thoughts would have inevitably turned to what they were going into – all that had gone before, and what might face them when they land. At that time, all flights from the UK landed in Kandahar, and the military personnel were then transported by air to Camp Bastion, the UK's main operating base, from which most are sent out to various smaller bases. Upon landing Harry, like everyone else, was given forty-eight hours for briefings, given live ammunition, morphine pens and dog tags. He was then taken by Chinook helicopter to Forward Operating Base Dwyer, a dusty and isolated outpost in the middle of Helmand province. Named after a young officer who had been killed the year before, the base is the size of four football pitches, ringed by a ditch, razor wire and heavy machine guns. Uncomfortable and austere, the soldiers slept in rough bunkers built from blast-proof wire mesh cages filled with rubble and topped with corrugated iron and sandbags. Like many of the men, Harry hung a glamour girl calendar above his bunk.

Harry acclimatized to his new desert surroundings, with their blazing hot days and temperatures of minus ten at night, while he was stationed in the middle of nowhere. Press Association photographer John Stillwell was selected to join Harry in Afghanistan on more than one occasion to record the prince at work, and recalls, 'It's incredibly hot, even in the winter, and it's incredibly desolate. It's a weird landscape – dead flat and then goes straight into mountains. All pretty inhospitable.'

The land is very sparsely populated, and the Afghan people mostly live in compounds around water, so there were a lot of people based around the Helmand River. Outside of those little pockets of civilization it is completely barren desert. 'The sand gets absolutely everywhere, recalls Stillwell. 'I had to leave a lot of equipment there because it was knackered.'

However, in the operations room Harry monitored the Taliban TV and later said it was one of the happiest times of his life – mucking in, no one caring that he was a prince, while the people he spoke to on the radio didn't know who he was. Those he worked with spoke highly of his work ethic, and his relaxed and easy-going nature. He was happy doing what he had been trained to do and it gave him a level of anonymity he very rarely experienced. Back home, he was constantly accompanied by protection officers wherever he went, which just wouldn't work in a war zone. In Afghanistan, SAS troopers were close at hand but they did not operate in the same capacity as his protection officers did back home. Harry explained later, 'It's very nice to be a normal person for once. I think this is about as normal as I am ever going to get. This is what it's all about, being here with the guys rather than being in a room with a bunch of officers. All my wishes have come true.'

It was a basic existence, covered in detail in the book *Harry's War* by Robert Jobson – there were no hot showers, only freezing cold water from a bag hung up in an outdoor wooden cubicle. Just like the others, Harry would lug around jerry cans of water, shaving once every three days and using the rounded ends of missile cases as shaving bowls. Like everyone else, he was rationed to one bottle of drinking water a day, which was airlifted in, and after that it was the metallic-tasting chlorinated water, often mixed with a flavoured powder called 'screech'.

For breakfast, he wolfed down a mixture of mashed biscuits, jam and margarine, and he snacked on peanuts, or biltong sent in the post from Chelsy. Main meals were boil-in-the-bag chicken tikka masala, bolognaise, or corned beef hash – all dosed with bottled sauces to add a bit of flavour. Harry said that he wished Jamie Oliver could transform the food as he had done with school dinners, 'Bangers and mash with gravy in a bag would be brilliant, awesome. I don't think you could screw that up, although I'm sure someone would manage to.'

When he wasn't in front of the monitor, it was a monotonous existence; weekends were no different to weekdays and so the days blended into each other. There were first aid drills and hours spent cleaning weapons and equipment. In his free time he flicked through lads mags, played poker and kicked a ball around made from loo rolls bound around with gaffer tape.

On Christmas Eve Harry asked to be posted to Gurkhas FOB Delhi in Garmsir. He explained, 'I asked the commanding officer if I could come down here and spend Christmas with the Gurkhas because I spent some time with them in England on exercise in Salisbury.' Garmsir was a bombed-out ghost town. There were smashed TV sets spilling out from shop fronts, and feral cats prowling. John Stillwell recalls, 'There were books, clothes and CDs just scattered all over the ground. I was taking a picture and something nudged my boot – I looked down and it was a load of Afghan bank notes!'

Back home, petrol-head Harry had been riding motorbikes for sometime, and was excited to find an abandoned old motorbike there. Stillwell remembers, 'Harry saw the bike just before it got dark and said, "I'm going to have a go on that at first light." I said, "You'll never get it going!" but they did manage. Another guy got on – Harry's superior – and I took a picture that didn't get shown as much. I preferred it because it was of Harry pushing someone else and it showed he was a team player. He wanted to take the bike back to Highgrove! Till someone pointed out to him that that would actually be called looting ...'

The base there was made up of a collection of bomb-ravaged buildings, shipping containers and army hardware with fortifications and observations posts at every turn. Men had added family photos, children's drawings, football flags and pictures torn from magazines of glamour models. Harry slept in a mortar-proof billet on a narrow camp bed with a mosquito net. There was a locker made from an old mortar shell box and a rug embroidered with pictures of tanks and hand grenades. Sunburnt Harry spent Christmas Day playing touch rugby in the bombed-out town with his new friends. He didn't get his father's Christmas card until February, but every week he was, like the other men, allowed thirty minutes on a satellite phone. He would speak to his family and Chelsy. He also kept a picture of her in his pocket.

Out on patrol, home was a Spartan armoured vehicle that contained everything they would need for days on end. They heated drinking water in a boiler built into the back door, and slept in shell scrapes – make-do shelters made by attaching tarpaulins to the vehicle – and warmed themselves with tea and coffee that tasted identical. In the Press Association interview he gave he said, 'I can't wait to get back and just sleep on a sofa. It's going to be ridiculous after bouncing around in a turret. My hips are bruised, my arse is bruised.' But he loved it, 'Just walking around with some of the locals or the Afghan National Police – they haven't got a clue who I am. They wouldn't know. It's fantastic.'

Harry was fearless, and Stillwell remembers, 'One time we were travelling through the desert and two guys in a car driving in front of us made us stop and were pointing. I think most people would say, "Go on, you go", but Harry marched straight over with the interpreter. The guy driving the tank we were in was sh***ing himself, saying, "Why has he gone over? I should be going over ..." These guys in the car could have had guns or a bomb. In the end it turned out one of them had a very bad leg and it was all bandaged up and the other one was taking him to hospital. It turned out to be nothing but there were a lot of people twitching when Harry goes marching over there. But that's Harry.'

The food was better at FOB Delhi because the Gurkhas would cook up delicious goat or chicken curries, and in his interview Harry explained, 'What am I missing the most? Nothing really. Music – we've got music. We've got light, we've got food, we've got non-alcoholic drink. No, I don't miss the booze if that's the next question … It's nice just to be here with the guys and just mucking in as one of the lads … It's bizarre. I'm out here now, haven't really had a shower for four days, haven't washed my clothes for a week, everything seems completely normal. I think this is about as normal as I'm going to get.' He was asked what his mother would have made of him being over there and said, 'Hopefully she'd be proud. She would be looking down having a giggle about the stupid things that I've been doing, like going left when I should have gone right … William sent me a letter saying how proud he reckons that she would be.'

The day before New Year's Eve, Harry was watching his monitor when the Taliban opened fire on a small British observation post, and he called in his first strike. It was his job to guide the aircraft in as they dropped their bombs and it was a success. Two days later, on 2 January 2008, he moved on once more, this time to a nineteenth-century fort not far from FOB Delhi, where he saw action again. Twenty Taliban were spotted moving towards Harry and his troop's position, and although the Gurkhas fired a missile, the Taliban kept advancing, so Harry seized a .50 calibre machine gun, aimed and fired. He had been making a video diary on his phone and a Gurkha soldier filmed him as he fired. After a thirty-minute battle they were victorious. Panning his camera-phone around the pock-marked ground, he commented: 'The whole place is just deserted. There are no roofs on any of the compounds, there are craters all over the place. It looks like something out of the Battle of the Somme.'

Around this time, an Australian magazine, *New Idea*, chose to ignore the embargo on Harry's deployment, and ran a story saying he was on the front line. Fortunately it wasn't picked up on straight away.

In the second week of January Harry was moved to FOB Edinburgh, seven kilometres from Taliban heartland. Musa Qala, a battle-battered town in the Sangin Valley, had just been taken by British and US troops after a battle lasting several weeks. The locals were living in fear as the Taliban had been burning their homes and destroying their crops and animals. It was here that Harry faced the horrors of war, when a Taliban rocket that was meant to strike Harry's vehicle instead hit the home of Afghan civilians. Harry's colleague Sergeant Deane Smith told the *Mail on Sunday*, 'Harry was there comforting a soldier as the charred remains of young children were removed. He also arranged for the wounded to be transferred from the battlefield to a military hospital.'

It was here that Harry also came closest to death when it was discovered that he was just one pace away from standing on an improvised exploding device, which he later laughed off on a cigarette break. He was good at keeping spirits up and on one occasion tied a pair of purple and yellow knickers to the front grille of an armoured vehicle. The underwear had been sent to him in the post, but as to speculation they were Chelsy's ... Harry wasn't saying.

Harry was all set to head up a group of seven men to capture the remote neighbouring village of Karis de Baba but unfortunately the story that had appeared in *New Idea* was then picked up by US blogger Matt Drudge and appeared on his blog 'The Drudge Report'. Once it was online, it spread around the world like wildfire, and Harry's cover was blown. He was pulled out on 29 February, told to pack his bags, and had just a few minutes to say goodbye to comrades and he was off home. He was angry, upset and frustrated, but on his flight to RAF Brize Norton were two critically injured servicemen who were semi-comatose for the entire flight. One had lost his left arm and right leg and the other had taken shrapnel to the neck. Later, Harry said, 'Those are the heroes … It was hard because it was a time when you wanted to talk to them and just find out how they were. Because a typical English or British soldier would just turn around and go, "Oh, I'm fine. I'm fine. I've lost my arm. I didn't like that arm anyway," or something like that. And the guy who took the shrapnel in the neck, when he was choking with blood, just grabbed the piece of shrapnel and said, "Put that in a pot, I want that as a souvenir." That's just the way it is and the bravery of the guys out there is just humbling, it's amazing.'

Harry landed on 1 March 2008, still wearing his fatigues covered with desert sand, devastated to be home before his men, and before he could complete the job he was sent to do. Charles and William were waiting for him at RAF Brize Norton. Asked how he felt, Harry said, 'Angry would be the wrong word to use, but I am slightly disappointed. I thought I could see it through to the end and come back with our guys.'

He had always had a prickly relationship with the media and couldn't hide his irritation. 'I am very disappointed that foreign websites have decided to run the story without consulting us. This is in stark contrast to the highly responsible attitude of the whole of the UK print and broadcast media.' Although adding, 'I was surprised by the way the British media kept to their side of the bargain … there was stuff they [the British media] did behind the scenes to stop stuff coming out, which was massively kind of them.' Prince Charles told the press it was a great relief that Harry was back, as well as paying tribute to all those who serve in the armed forces.

Harry was allowed three weeks' leave before he rejoined his unit, and was promoted to Lieutenant on 1 April. He made the most of his freedom and went on holiday – returning to the Okavango Delta in Botswana with Chelsy. Once more, they stayed on the *Kubu Queen*, at night climbing a tin ladder to their tent on the houseboat's roof and each morning rising late and cooking breakfast on a small gas cooker, before sailing up the crocodile-infested river with a few beers. This time they took a speedboat out to a hippo watering hole, which Harry drove on the way back.

*

The verdict of the inquest into Diana's death finally came through in April 2008. The jury released an official statement that said that Diana and Dodi, along with driver Henri Paul, were unlawfully killed by the 'grossly negligent driving of the following vehicles and of the Mercedes', adding that additional factors were, 'the impairment of the judgement of the driver of the Mercedes through alcohol', and the death of the deceased was 'caused or contributed to by the fact that the deceased [were] not wearing seat belts and the fact the Mercedes struck a pillar in the Alma Tunnel, rather then colliding with something else'. Harry and William released a joint statement thanking the jury, the coroner Lord Justice Scott Baker and Trevor Rees, who was the only survivor of the crash. 'Finally, the two of us would like to express our most profound gratitude to all those who fought so desperately to save our mother's life on that tragic night.'

After ten and a half years, the case was finally over, and

that spring was also a time for family celebration as Harry and William's cousin Peter Phillips was getting married. William flew himself and Harry to Peter's stag do on the Isle of Wight by helicopter, which was questioned as a waste of tax-payers' money, however it had been cleared by senior officials and was seen as a legitimate exercise to help with William's training.

So, what happens on a royal stag party? On this occasion, the stags, who included Zara's boyfriend Mike Tindall, dressed in cricket whites with 'Pedro's Stag' written on the front of their shirts and their names on the back – 'Wills' for William and 'Hazza' for Harry. They set Peter challenges including carrying round an inflatable doll, played cricket and went to local pub The Anchor to listen to live music and play pool. 'They were very polite to staff – it was nice to have them here,' said the pub's manager. 'There was a large group here and they were all well behaved.' The next day they went to Cowes Marina and boarded a yacht for a day's sailing. Peter was made to wear a purple lycra catsuit and had glasses and a moustache drawn on his face with black marker pen. Harry also befriended another stag group dressed as pirates in a local bar.

In May, Harry received a service medal from his aunt the Princess Royal, Colonel-in-Chief of the Blues and Royals. Chelsy was seated next to William, with Prince Charles on his other side. Four years into their tempestuous relationship, and it was the first time Chelsy had attended an official engagement. Also in May was Peter Phillips' wedding, at which Chelsy was introduced to the Queen. As well as making strides in his relationship, Harry was also becoming increasingly involved in all things military. For some time Harry and William had been interested in the recovery and care of injured service people – both brothers have friends who have been injured in combat, and know people who have been killed serving their country. When a new charity Help for Heroes had been launched the previous autumn, it was only a matter of days before the two brothers were publicly showing their support by wearing the charity's wristbands and making enquiries about how they could help. They came up with an initiative called City Salute, a concert performance held in front of St Paul's Cathedral that raised £1 million for Help for Heroes, the Headley Court Defence Medical Rehabilitation Centre, and the Soldiers, Sailors, Airmen and Families Association, which also supports injured service people and their families.

Help for Heroes founder Bryn Parry was impressed with Harry's ability to connect with all those he meets. 'I can't over-emphasize how good he is at getting on with and understanding the guys,' says Parry. 'And he's hugely perceptive with the families. When he meets a mum or a wife or a child, he always seems to be able to gauge the right thing to say to them to make them feel better. They all go away feeling the better for meeting him and I think he does too. He has an enthusiasm and an irreverent sense of humour, and always knows if he's met someone before.'

In July, Harry returned to Lesotho along with twenty members of the Blues and Royals and they all helped to build a children's school – pushing wheelbarrows and filling trenches. In the autumn he headed once more to Suffield in Canada for further training. In the wilderness of the vast Canadian prairie he proved that not only was he a skilled soldier, but had also become a respected and honourable leader of men. He was there as troop commander and his gunner was the openly gay twenty-one-year-old James Wharton, with whom he had trained before deployment to Iraq.

Wharton makes no secret of his sexuality, however there are many other soldiers in the military who are closeted. In his book *Out in the Army* James recounts his career in the army as an out gay man. On one occasion James spent the night with a fellow soldier and the next day was confronted by six infantry sergeants who angrily accused him of spreading false rumours about their colleague and threatened to 'batter' him. Wharton went to find Harry, his superior. 'I told him "I think I'm going to be murdered by the infantry!" I climbed into the turret and talked Harry through exactly what had happened. He had a look of complete bewilderment on his face. I couldn't stop the tears from welling up in my eyes. He said, "Right. I'm going to sort this s*** out once and for all." Harry confronted the men. 'I could see he wasn't holding back,' said Wharton. 'He came back ten minutes later and told me the problem had been "sorted". He told me, "I know one of the officers and we cleared everything up. I also told those other lads to back the f*** off, too."'

Wharton believes that the way Harry handled the men and their homophobia was the first time an officer had made such a bold move, saying: 'It was 2008. I have to say I thought his actions were pretty forward-moving for the time in the military, particularly surrounding gay equality. Today I would expect young officers to be generally forward moving, but in 2008 it was out of the ordinary.'

While they were on exercise one day in their tank, Harry and Wharton were enjoying some banter, 'Harry insisted that he's a gay icon,' recalls James. 'I was jokingly disagreeing with him, teasing him and saying, "You're such a homophobe." He had this look of utter disbelief on his face and said that all his life he'd had gay friends. I'm not sure who he was referring to but he said, "One of our closest friends is gay and he's been around us all our lives." I think sexuality just isn't a big thing for him. He's a completely modern prince.'

As well as having gay friends, Wharton believes that it was his mother Diana's influence that led Harry to be the level-headed and accepting man he is today. 'I do a lot of voluntary work for the Terence Higgins Trust and I know that Diana would often bring her boys along to see what work was going on. I've seen a picture of her sat next to an AIDS sufferer, with Harry sat the other side, and Harry's probably six or seven years old, so I think it's quite deeply seated in him to understand and be caring.' Wharton continues that during their down time, despite the aforementioned breaking down of boundaries, and the fact they talked openly on a number of personal subjects, the subject of Diana never came up. 'The boys were very good and people didn't generally overstep the mark. There was an invisible line in our minds and we wouldn't cross it.' Although a little humour regarding another family member was welcome. 'We were watching an Arsenal match on TV one night,' Wharton remembers. 'Someone said, "Who does the Queen support?" and Harry jokingly said "Arsenal of course."'

However, not all those whom Harry came across knew how to tread that fine line, and despite his relaxed informal relationship with his men, Harry took action when someone went too far. 'I remember a situation when one of the boys wanted to go to the horse-racing at Royal Ascot,' recalls Wharton. 'He couldn't get tickets, and he thought it would be a good idea to ask Harry if he could help. I believe that was the line crossed. I think something was said about that from above.'

Wharton and Harry, however, maintained a good relationship throughout their training and James still has nothing but praise for his former leader, however he also believes he was able to offer something to Harry. 'Our tank had broken down for the millionth time, we were all sitting around pissed off, we all needed

Above: Prince Harry sits in his room in his final year at Eton College, May 2003.
Below: Posing with his horse, Guardsman, while working as a jackaroo on a cattle ranch in Tooloombilla, Australia in November 2003.

Above: Harry went to Lesotho to launch his charity, Sentebale, in 2006. Co-founded with Prince Seeiso of Lesotho, it aims to help vulnerable children and those orphaned by AIDS.

Below: A proud grandmother smiles warmly at her grandson as she inspects soldiers at their passing-out Sovereign's Parade at Sandhurst Military Academy in April 2006.

Above: William and Harry introduce the 'Concert for Diana' on 1 July 2007, held in honour of Diana, Princess of Wales and timed to coincide with what would have been her forty-fifth birthday.

Below: With his long-time girlfriend Chelsy Davy in May 2008.

Above: In Afghanistan in 2008. *Left:* On patrol. *Right:* Enjoying a lighter moment.
Below: In March 2011 Harry joined the Walking with the Wounded expedition for their final days of preparation on the island of Spitsbergen before the team set off for the North Pole on foot.

Left: A very happy day as the Groom and his Best Man enter Westminster Abbey on William's wedding day, 29 April 2011.

Below: The Duke and Duchess of Cambridge and Prince Harry attend the *Sun* Military Awards at the Imperial War Museum in December 2011.

As part of The Queen's Diamond Jubilee Tour in 2012, Harry visited the Bahamas, Belize and Jamaica. *Above left*: a formal occasion at Government House in Nassau. *Above right*: dancing rather more informally on a visit to a charity project in Jamaica. *Below:* 'Beating' the world's fastest man, Usain Bolt, on his home turf.

Above: With Kate and William at the 2012 London Olympics, enjoying yet another victory in the velodrome.

Below left: The now notorious visit to Las Vegas that gained Harry headlines around the world.

Below right: Harry's girlfriend Cressida Bonas with Princess Eugenie at Thomas Van Straubenzee's wedding in June 2013.

Above: Harry served as an Apache Helicopter Pilot/Gunner with 662 Sqd Army Air Corps at Camp Bastion, Afghanistan, from September 2012 until January 2013.
Below: Harry plays a game of Uckers in the VHR (Very High Ready-ness) tent with fellow pilots at Camp Bastion.

a shower and we had to pass the time,' remembers Wharton. 'I always used to carry cooking oil and Spam at the bottom of my kit, because when you've been out in the hills for five nights and all you've had is the bog-standard rations that they give you, fried Spam and Tabasco sauce really cheers people up. So we fried it and we talked. I think he was bit amazed to see me pull it out of my bag and said, "What the hell is that?" I said, "Do not judge this until you've tasted it!" And he was delighted. We went back to base two days later to have a shower and pick up some fresh supplies, and when we got back to the bus he delightedly turned up exclaiming that he'd bought a load of Spam and he had it in his bag. It's the simple things …'

*

On Harry's return to the UK he attended the premiere for the new Bond film, *Quantum of Solace*. It was in a line-up during the glittering black-tie event that Harry showed both his weakness and his strength to Help for Heroes founder Bryn Parry. 'When he saw me he grinned and said, "I think I've made a faux pas …"' recalls Parry. "I just said to Daniel Craig that I thought Sean Connery was the best James Bond!" Harry was laughing at himself and realized what he'd said as soon as he said it. What I liked about that is that we all say the wrong thing sometimes – it's very human – and Harry has the humanity and the normality to tell someone else about it and say "look I've just made a fool of myself", which immediately puts people at their ease.'

When he and William had been invited to attend, they decided they wanted to include the wounded, so the red carpet was lined with members of the armed forces and wounded veterans. Proceeds raised went to the British Legion and Help for Heroes.

Before the end of the month Harry was back in Africa, this time with William, as the adventure-loving brothers were taking part in a charity motorbike race from Port Edward on KwaZulu-Natal's southern coast down to Port Elizabeth, organized by an adventure travel company called Global Enduro. The brothers both rode motorbikes back home, and Harry was driving an £8,000 Triumph back in the UK. 'We never really get to spend any time together,' he said before the race. 'It's not just a bimble across the countryside … We're expecting to fall off many a time. We've got a secret bet with everybody else about who's going to fall off between us.' It certainly wasn't a 'bimble' – their group travelled 100 miles a day in 40 degrees heat, helping to raise £300,000 for children's charities in South Africa, including Sentebale, Nelson Mandela's Children's Fund and UNICEF. One day one rider fell in the water as they were crossing a river and Harry jumped in to save him – earning himself the 'Spirit of the Day' award. Simon Smith, the founder of Global Enduro, accompanied them, saying later, 'They were both fantastic riders and didn't run from anything. They asked us to treat them as one of the group and that's what we did. They mucked in with chores and shared a beer and food around the barbecue.'

Global Enduro billed themselves as, 'A passionate like-minded tribe of people who come together to co-create life-affirming experiences. We dramatically improve the lives of the people we meet en route, through raising money and awareness for causes we believe in and that is why we are truly, "At the Heart of Adventure"'. However, in 2013 the firm went into administration, while still owing money to Sentebale and other charities – a matter that is still being resolved.

After getting down and dirty on motorbikes for charity with his brother, Harry headed home. Chelsy was back in the UK and based in London while she interned for solicitors Farrer & Company, who have acted for the Queen. Cracks started to appear in their relationship around this time but, after Harry spent his Christmas as usual at Sandringham, he and Chelsy headed off to Africa once more to welcome in the New Year. This time with her family on the relaxed and beautiful tropical island of Mauritius, located off the coast of Africa in the Indian Ocean.

*

After slowly building their team for the last few years, in January 2009, with Harry aged twenty-four and William twenty-six, the Queen allowed the princes to officially set up their own private household, which was a big step into the public arena, and also gave them some independence. Jamie Lowther-Pinkerton and Helen Asprey stayed on in their roles, while, at Harry's suggestion, the role of press secretary was filled by Miguel Head, the MoD press officer who had helped coordinate Harry's trip to Afghanistan. Sir David Manning, the former British Ambassador to the US, was appointed as a part-time advisor. The princes would be visiting countries all over the world with very different cultures, political and economical positions, and he would be able to advise them in all matters.

Also in January, Harry and William both became patrons of the Henry van Straubenzee Memorial Fund, which had been set up by Henry's parents to raise money for projects and schools in Uganda. The launch was at the Troubadour Club in London and both princes spoke. Harry said, 'As some of you know, Henry was one of my greatest friends and his death was truly shocking. Henry would have been so proud of his family for what they are doing in his name. Everything that's going on in Uganda and the way they are carrying his memory on is remarkable.'

January, however, seemed to be a jinxed month for Harry as, following January 2002 when the story was run about his underage drinking, and January 2005 when he was photographed in the Nazi uniform, this time, in 2009, footage was released of him three years earlier when he was at Sandhurst on a training exercise in Cyprus. Harry and his fellow Officer Cadets were all at the airport and many of them were crashed out on the floor in their army fatigues with their heads covered so they could sleep. But Harry was awake, filming them all on his camera-phone and narrating all the while. During the footage as he panned around he said, 'Anyone else here? Ah, our little Paki friend,' referring to Captain Ahmed Raza Khan. On a night training exercise he'd said to another soldier: 'F*** me! You look like a raghead.' Captain Khan said he took no offence, but Harry still apologized via his press office, who released a statement reading: 'Prince Harry fully understands how offensive this term can be, and is extremely sorry for any offence his words might cause. However on this occasion three years ago, Prince Harry used the term without any malice and as a nickname about a highly popular member of his platoon. There is no question that Prince Harry was in any way seeking to insult his friend.'

CHAPTER TWELVE

'The Devil's dance floor'

Leaving behind the recent furore, Harry headed to the Hampshire countryside for the next part of his army training, enrolling on an eighteen-month helicopter attack pilot course with the Army Air Corps in Middle Wallop. He was on a break with Chelsy who was homesick and felt neglected by him, and who had changed her Facebook relationship status to 'not in one'.

His course began with four weeks of intensive tutorials in the classroom before he was allowed in the cockpit, and he struggled. He was also enrolled on an army diversity course to make him more racially aware. He divided his time between RAF Cranwell, where William trained (as Charles had before them), and RAF Barkston Heath, both in Lincolnshire. It meant lots of hard work, no time for girlfriends and no drinking, because trainees couldn't drink for ten hours before flying. For £150 a month he rented a small room with a single bed and an en-suite bathroom. He took classes from 9.00 until 5.30 and struggled with theory, saying later, 'The flying is fantastic, but there are times I've thought I'm not really cut out for this mentally. It's really intense. I knew it was going to be tough, but I never thought it would be this tough. I hope I've got the physical skills to fly a helicopter. But there are exams and everything. I can't do maths – I gave that up when I left school.' He was being trained to fly a Firefly, a small fixed-wing aircraft. He set his heart on flying an Apache but admitted, 'Brain capacity? I don't know if I've got it for the Apache.'

The Boeing AH-64 Apache is a four-blade, twin-engine attack helicopter which was first flown in 1975. It was developed for the US Army's advanced helicopter attack programme, and named the Apache in keeping with the US Army's tradition of using American Indian tribal names for their helicopters. Those in service in the UK have Rolls-Royce engines, and they are designed to hunt and destroy in all weathers. Their pilots are said to be the best of the best. It was this beast that Harry had his heart set on flying.

In March 2009, on Sentebale's third anniversary, he made a speech. He wrote it himself, and spoke from the heart, also paying tribute to his mother: 'Prince Seeiso and I founded Sentebale in memory of our mothers. They worked tirelessly to help the deprived and the afflicted and in our own way we aspire to follow their great example. Unless we help Lesotho … these wonderful people will be decimated and their society destroyed.'

By early May, Harry had graduated from fixed-wing aircraft to the Squirrel helicopter and was about to join William at the Defence Helicopter Flying School at RAF Shawbury near Shrewsbury. He had also won the Horsa Trophy, which is awarded by instructors and fellow trainee pilots to 'the man you would most want on your squadron'. He was now finally training to fly Apache attack helicopters.

In May he played in a charity polo match in New York in aid of Sentebale. He arrived on 29 May and visited Ground Zero, where he met families who had lost loved ones in the 11 September attacks. He also planted a tree at the British Memorial Garden in downtown Manhattan. Another visit was to the Children's Zone in Harlem, where he raced round an assault course with youngsters popping balloons in a relay race.

Harry was proving to be an asset to the royal family – including in America, where 'Harry mania' was taking hold. The girls loved him, and the phrase 'Harry hunter' started to take off in reference to girls who would try to track him down in the hopes of snaring him.

In June, Harry and William gave a joint interview at RAF Shawbury, where they were living together in a rented cottage near the air base. The cottage was so small, that one visitor remarked there was 'hardly room to swing a cat'. From the interview, it was obvious how well they got on, as they talked over each other, teasing, laughing, joking and making sideswipes, as Harry always tried to get the last word in. William revealed, 'Bearing in mind I cook for him and feed him every day, I think he's done rather well. He does a bit of the washing up and then he leaves it in the sink and then he comes back in the morning and I have to wash it up.' Harry shook his head, while grinning, 'Lies!' William also revealed, 'He snores a lot as well and keeps me up all night long,' before Harry groaned, 'They're going to think we're sharing a bed now!' He spoke of the intensive training he'd been undertaking, again referencing his dyslexia, saying ''Exams have never been my favourite and I always knew that I was going to find it harder than most people.' William then sang his brother's praises, saying how well he was doing on the course, and when Harry started teasing him again, said indignantly, 'I've said something nice, now you can say something nice,' Harry hugged him and said, 'He's great!'

*

In the months since their break-up, Harry was still thinking about Chelsy but he had accompanied his friend Sam Branson to Natalie Imbruglia's fancy-dress birthday party, where he struck up a close friendship with the singer. He also had a brief fling with TV presenter Caroline Flack, whom he had been introduced to at a charity poker tournament by their mutual friend Natalie Pinkham. Chelsy had also dated someone else – a property developer called Dan Philipson. However, it was clear that neither Harry nor Chelsy were ready to forget about each other, and neither relationship worked out. In July, Chelsy completed her law course and deferred her job as a trainee solicitor in order to take another gap year, and by August she and Harry were back together. To celebrate his twenty-fifth birthday, he took her and a group of friends back to the Okavango Delta for another trip aboard the *Kubu Queen*.

Now they were young men, Harry and William were a force to be reckoned with. They had their own household and staff, they were taking on charity patronages and had pioneered their charity forum, and then, in September, they decided to set up their own charity – the Foundation of Prince William and Prince Harry (now called the Royal Foundation of the Duke and Duchess of Cambridge and Prince Harry). The foundation was launched as an umbrella charity to kick-start certain projects and cast light on others, while also giving them their own money to distribute as they wished. There were to be three main areas that the charity would focus on: helping young people; raising awareness and support for the armed forces; and conservation.

Harry and Chelsy welcomed in the New Year in Mauritius with her parents once more, and at the beginning of 2010 the on-off lovebirds moved in together, sharing a £1.5 million three-bedroom home in London's Belgravia, one of the wealthiest districts in the world. It was the start of many firsts for Harry, as he and William had their first official portrait painted by Nicky Philipps, which was unveiled in January in the National Portrait Gallery. Harry commented he was 'more ginger in there than I am in real life'.

Harry then went to Barbados at the end of the month to launch the annual Sentebale Polo Cup, which from that point on would always be a part of his fundraising calendar. While in the Caribbean, Harry also hosted a fundraising dinner in aid of the humanitarian effort in Haiti. Neither he nor William had undertaken their own royal overseas tour as yet, but they were both beginning to take on more engagements, including those abroad. Such engagements were designed to help draw attention to the issues that were important to the country being visited, and following the terrible earthquake in Haiti just a few days before, raising funds was of countrywide importance.

The inaugural Sentebale Polo Cup was a huge success, however Harry experienced sadness on the polo field four months later, when he was playing in a charity match in Coworth Park with William. Harry had just played a chukka in the second half when he realized that his ten-year-old pony, Drizzle, was struggling. He noticed that she was not running comfortably and decided to take her out of the match. Sadly, within minutes, she suffered a heart attack and died. The pony had been a family favourite for a long time, and Charles used to ride her before Harry. The young prince was in tears as he smoked a cigarette, and decided not to stay for the socializing afterwards.

*

Harry was presented with his wings on 7 May by his father, as Chelsy looked on. It meant he was accepted to fly Apaches. According to someone who knows him, 'There's no side to Harry, he doesn't expect special treatment and the guys all love him. He really struggled with the academic stuff but put his head down and forced his way through it and now he's one of the best Apache pilots of the lot.' Another adds, 'He flies an Apache better than anybody else on his course. You don't get to be an Apache pilot unless you're in the top ten per cent and if you're heading the course, you're a really exceptional flyer.'

There had been whisperings about Harry's capabilities in the course of much of his studies – from Eton onwards. However, one thing was for sure, the MoD would not send someone to war flying valuable equipment and putting lives at risk, were he not up to the job.

Harry and William then joined forces to travel through their beloved Africa for their first set of joint overseas engagements. Over five days in June they visited Botswana, Lesotho and South Africa. In Botswana, the princes saw first-hand the work of Tusk Trust, of whom William is a patron. The organization aims to preserve the endangered wildlife and educate the people in the local area about conservation. In Lesotho, the princes visited projects supported by Sentebale. There Harry and William were asked to participate in a custom where they wrote down some of their hopes and dreams, and Harry wrote: 'professional surfer', 'wildlife photographer', 'helicopter pilot', and 'to live in Africa'.

In South Africa they rounded off their trip by supporting the FA's bid to host the 2018 FIFA World Cup. William is president of the FA, and the brothers joined a reception to celebrate the 2010 FIFA World Cup in South Africa. The princes also attended the match between England and Algeria, which ended in a disappointing 0–0 draw. Because Harry already knew David Beckham, the brothers went to the England team's dressing room afterwards. The superstar footballer and William were also to become good friends, and he would later socialize and work with both brothers, even popping up on both William and Harry's first overseas tours, attending a reception with William in LA, and providing a video message for the GREAT event that Harry attended in Brazil.

In August, Harry was ecstatic to learn that he had passed his ground school exam, a part of his Apache helicopter-training course. He admitted the training was likely to be one of the biggest challenges of his life. A spokesman said, 'Flying comes more naturally to Harry than the mathematical and scientific papers that have marked the start of the course.'

Around the time of his twenty-sixth birthday, he and Chelsy split once again, and while she went back to South Africa to continue her career there, he was seen partying at an Olympics Ball at the Grosvenor House Hotel before leaving at 3 a.m. to carry on partying at Raffles on the King's Road with his cousin Zara, leaving with a number scrawled on the palm of his hand.

In October, Harry quietly attended a Help for Heroes concert, with performances from Gary Barlow and Robbie Williams, The Saturdays and Pixie Lott. He stayed in the background as he wanted the attention to be firmly on the wounded community. Help for Heroes' Bryn Parry recalls, 'Harry said he'd like to come but not as a royal guest, so in the royal box the front row was filled with injured service people, but he came in afterwards and sat at the back, out of sight. He did all of his meeting of them out of camera shot. I always think this is the difference between members of the royal family and politicians. What the family do publicly is sometimes what they are required to do, and what they do privately is what they want to do. A lot of their business is done quietly, behind the scenes, that no one sees.'

*

While Harry and Chelsy were increasingly more off than on, his brother's relationship with Kate Middleton had gone from strength to strength. 'You've got a sister!' was the way William broke the news to Harry that his long-term girlfriend had accepted his marriage proposal. 'A younger brother or sister would have been nicer, but to have a big sister is obviously very, very nice,' was Harry's public response to the news. Harry was impetuous and bold, while Kate was measured and subtle but the pair got on very well and Harry has always been very protective of her. He added, 'I've got to know Kate pretty well, but now that she's becoming part of the family I'm really looking forward to getting her under my wing – or she'll be taking me under her wing probably … She's a fantastic girl, she really is. My brother's very lucky, and she's very lucky to have my brother. I think the two of them are a perfect match.'

In February, he was back in Chelsy's arms and they had a few secret nights out in London hot spots. In the last week of March, Harry, along with Guy Pelly, organized William's stag do, which was held in Hartland Abbey in Devon. The former monastery dates back to the twelfth century and is surrounded by gardens, alongside a private section of coastline. The house is owned by the Stucley family, whose son, George, is a close friend of William, and it was used in the 2007 BBC adaptation of *Sense and Sensibility*. On the Saturday morning the young men had a hearty breakfast before heading outside for an hour's clay pigeon shooting. They had a competition to see who was the best shot, and polished off several bottles of vintage port. Over the course of the weekend they also took advantage of the sunny weather – spending the afternoon surfing at Spekes Mill, a beauty spot a couple of miles to the south.

In March, Harry continued his transition from cheeky little boy and impish teenager to dashing blade, when he became a *GQ* magazine cover star. He gave an interview and posed for a set of pictures shot by David Bailey to publicize the Walking With The Wounded expedition to the North Pole, which he would be taking part in, while a donation from each issue sold would go to the charity. Walking With The Wounded was set up by former Royal Green Jackets officer Ed Parker and his old Sandhurst classmate Simon Daglish, after Ed's nephew Harry lost both his legs when he stepped on an improvised explosive device while serving in Afghanistan. The money raised was to be used for the re-training and rehabilitation of injured British service personnel.

Their aim was to trek unaided to the North Pole, and so the selection process was rigorous. The first stage involved interviewing potential candidates in London, before taking a shortlist of successful applicants to the Arctic to assess whether they were physically able to go on the arduous journey. After that, Ed and Simon carefully decided that the four injured servicemen embarking on the expedition with them would be Captain Guy Disney, Private Jaco van Gass, Sergeant Steve Young and Captain Martin Hewitt, along with training guide

Henry Cookson and polar guide Inge Solheim.

Harry was involved as a patron from the very beginning, but it was only at the press launch that he stated publicly that he would like to join them. Ed Parker was completely taken aback, and recalls, 'We were just asking for patronage and I don't even think we considered it was worth asking him to come along, but at the press launch, very much unplanned, he said, "And I hope I might be able to come along too …" and it caught us by surprise. Yes, was the answer! It gave the whole thing a completely different momentum. Raising sponsorship was significantly easier and it made it more fun. For the guys going, knowing Harry would be there added a bit of fizz to it, which was great.'

As soon as the prince was involved, it meant that there was considerably more interest than there may otherwise have been. They were now to be accompanied by a small BBC film crew to shoot a two-part documentary called *Harry's Arctic Heroes*.

It was to be a challenging expedition. As well as the extreme cold, there was the fact that the team would be trekking purely on ice. The Antarctic is made up of land but the Arctic consists of slabs of frozen ocean. At the time, Inge Solheim explained the perils, 'You have no idea how different the pole is from everything else on this planet. The old Norwegian explorers called it "The Devil's dance floor". It will just slap you … You can walk ten miles in one day, pitch your tent overnight and the ice will have drifted you back eleven miles in the opposite direction.'

The year before, only two unsupported expeditions to the North Pole succeeded and those were by able-bodied teams. The mission was so dangerous that Harry did not even tell the Queen beforehand. 'My father obviously knew I was coming out here and so did my brother but I kind of kept it quiet,' he explained during the documentary. 'My grandparents and the rest of the family probably think I'm completely mad.'

They would be justified for thinking it. The previous year Harry had been burned, battered and shot at in the Afghan desert, and this year he would be up against minus 50-degree temperatures and 110-mile-an-hour winds. Each member of the team were to pull everything they needed in pulks (sleds) and were armed against polar bears in case of attack. They would be skiing for two hours and then breaking for ten minutes, skiing for two hours, breaking for ten minutes – all day every day. It was an extraordinary challenge for Harry and the other able-bodied members of the team, let alone the injured men.

Harry wasn't able to go for the whole trip as he had a certain royal wedding to attend, so he hadn't done as much training as the others. He was in good shape, however, and when he joined the rest of the team at the beginning of their journey in Longyearbyen, Norway, he tried cross-country skiing for the first time, luckily taking to it easily. The entire team were all acclimatizing to the cold, and had to be ready to fly to their kick-off point at a moment's notice, as soon as the conditions were right. Their lives would be in their pulks, as they would be totally alone when they got out into the Arctic wilderness, so they had to check and recheck that they had packed everything they needed. As Ed Parker points out: 'If you look round on day one and there's no loo roll, you can't pop to Tesco's to pick up another one. So you pack and unpack, and repack, and in the middle of the night you think, I've forgotten something ...'

The pulks weighed between eighty and one hundred kilos and carried fuel, cookers, tents, clothes, medical kit, weapons, radio and toiletries. All the food was dehydrated and they would add melted snow to rehydrate it, as well as using melted snow as their drinking water. 'The food is not great,' says Parker. 'It was all about the calories you slam in.' The team would tuck into chilli con carne, pasta bolognaise, or a generic chicken dish, however, Parker adds, 'To be honest with you if you closed your eyes you wouldn't know which one was which. Apart from the chilli because the kidney beans were like bullets.'

They all took their own additions to liven up the meals, including dried herbs or chilli flakes. Tabasco was a no-no as it would freeze solid. 'It's all high-calorie specialist expedition food,' explains Parker. 'You're burning a lot of calories in the day so you have to eat food that has the right balance of calories, fat and protein. We'd been working with nutritionists at GlaxoSmithKline who'd made us a special high-calorie Horlicks mix.'

Meanwhile, the conditions meant that there was a different approach to personal hygiene as well. 'You don't wash with water,' explains Parker. 'You use sanitizing gel to clean your hands, and keep a small bottle next to your skin so it doesn't freeze. Then, in the evening, you use wet-wipes, which again you keep against your skin, and wipe your nooks and crannies.'

On 13 April the conditions were right and the team headed to the ice-station Barneo in Russia on a two-hour flight, and even that was dicier than the team were expecting. Parker recalls, 'We landed in a white-out and if you land in a white-out on a white runway the pilots don't really know where they're going. When the left wing tip touched the ice first I remember one of Harry's protection officers looking at me with blind panic. The pilot turned round after we'd landed and wiped his brow and went "whew"'. It was around 4.30 a.m., with the strange glow of a place which doesn't ever get completely dark at that time of year, when they were delivered by helicopter to their kicking-off point. 'I remember watching the helicopter becoming a little black dot,' recalls Parker. 'And then we realized we were on our own. It was the first time we had been in the real, grown-up cold. I think we were all a bit bemused that first ten-fifteen minutes. Here we were and it wasn't quite how we'd expected it. Our guide told us to get our tents up and try to get some sleep, but I think everyone was buzzing with adrenaline and so no one slept very well.'

Their new surroundings were unlike anything the team had seen before. Parker says, 'It's the most beautiful place I've ever seen. In pictures it looks flat and white but the ice is broken and the sun refracts through it so you get the most extraordinary colours. It's blues and reds and greens and oranges, and it's staggeringly beautiful.' However, there was danger lurking not far at all beneath their boots. 'But then you have this very unnerving feeling that you're only standing on a fairly thin sheet of ice,' he continued. 'It's not dry land. Below you is four km of black old ocean. After a while I just imagined I was on dry land. Every now and then you come across an area where the ice has split open and there's water and I just used to imagine it was a stream or a river depending on how wide it was.'

All in the group felt honoured to be there though, and Parker explains, 'It's not a place where many people have been, so just being there felt like an enormous privilege. And being there with a small group of people you had chosen to be with – no one around that you don't want there – it had a wonderful feel to it. Every now and then that is. Most of the time it was bloody miserable!'

It was on the second day of the trek that Harry faced his most dangerous moment when he stepped through wafer-thin ice and partially slipped into the water. It was a reminder of the perilousness of their surroundings. 'You can hear the ice groaning and creaking,' recalls Parker. 'You're on top of an ocean, so the currents are moving the ice about and it's a bit unnerving at night, when it sounds like a rifle shot when two bits of ice part.' The other biggest problem was the cold. 'It's the fact it never goes away,' explains Parker. 'If you take it for granted it will come and damage you. I was a bit conscious that we had the third in line to the throne there and it wouldn't be very cool if he came back with ice and snow damage, but he's a grown-up and he's quite able to look after himself. Although he did get a white ear one day.' Luckily, Inge Solheim noticed the early stages of frostbite and saved the royal lobe.

It was here as well as at the front line that Harry was without his protection officers and he felt completely free. Parker says, 'He was just like everyone else. He's got a lot of grit about him. I didn't notice he was there as a prince. I just noticed he was there as the eighth team member. You could turn round to him and say, "Oi, get that, fill this, push that," and he would also turn round to one of us and say "do this, do that". He's now a close friend of the four guys who went with us. He is such a normal, ordinary, approachable man, there's no barrier you have to break through to find the real him.' Regretfully, Harry left the rest of the men to complete their challenge as he flew back to the UK for a wedding that had the entire country in a state of excitement.

*

On the morning of 29 April 2011, when the two princes stepped out of their claret Bentley, immaculate in their full military regalia, the crowd went wild. William wore the iconic scarlet tunic of the Irish Guards, of whom he was Colonel of the First Battalion, while Harry wore the uniform of a Captain of the Household Cavalry. Some had been camping around Westminster Abbey for three days, and although the Beckhams, Sir Elton John and Guy Ritchie had already arrived, there was nothing like the arrival of the two brothers to herald the approaching start of the ceremony.

People gathered in their thousands, fuelled by the infectious carnival atmosphere, thermos flasks of tea, bottles of wine and scotch eggs. The first few pop-up tents had started appearing on the pavements before the big day on the Friday, and before long whole encampments were building up all around the Abbey. There were tables and chairs set up, full-scale picnic feasts, campers in wedding outfits, cardboard royal family masks and a King Charles spaniel in a veil.

The night before the wedding, Harry stayed over at Clarence House with his brother, father and Camilla. The streets around Clarence House were also thronged with campers, and as dusk fell, William decided he would like to go out among them all and meet some of the people who had made the effort to be there. Harry was keen to go too. At 8.30 the brothers, dressed in jeans and jumpers, strolled out among the surprised crowds to chat to them. Harry invited himself into one camper's tent, and asked if another had drinks and nibbles. They then went back to Clarence House and had dinner with their father and Camilla, and while William retired early in preparation for his big day, Harry headed over to the Goring Hotel, which had been booked out exclusively by the bride-to-be's family, the Middletons. After drinks with Kate's sister Pippa, on-off girlfriend Chelsy and some of their friends, he called it a night around 3 a.m. by clambering onto a balcony, jumping off and loping back to Clarence House to get some sleep.

William and Kate had wanted their big day to be something for the whole country to celebrate, but also wanted to put their own personal touches on it wherever they could. One of the breaks with tradition was by having Harry as best man instead of the previous royal tradition of a 'supporter'. After the brothers had arrived and walked down the aisle together, with William chatting to the Middletons and Harry exchanging a few words with their mother's side of the family, they slipped off to a side chapel, where they remained until just before Kate left the Goring. It was Harry who turned to watch as Kate appeared at the bottom of the aisle and, beaming, reported back to William, 'Right, she is here now ... well, she looks beautiful, I can tell you that!'

The ceremony was watched by two billion people around the world, and many hoped that Harry would hook up with Kate's attractive younger sister Pippa, whom he escorted back down the aisle. However, Pippa attended the ceremony with her then boyfriend Alex Loudon, and Harry's guest was Chelsy.

Following the more formal lunchtime wedding buffet attended by heads of state, the evening reception was much more relaxed, and the couple were surrounded by their family and friends. The atmosphere was described as 'electric' and 'buzzing' by a female band member who performed. After dinner, Harry had the room in fits of laughter with his best man's speech, and his comic timing and brilliant one-liners were commented on. He had said beforehand, 'I'm doing the speech with a couple of his friends, so I will take the mickey out of him ... the speech will be like any normal best man's speech ... people will know the good times and the bad times that he's had since he was a nipper.'

The 'other two' he was referring to were Thomas van Straubenzee and James Meade. It was reported that Harry spoke of being beaten up by his brother and shot by air rifles, he teased William about his romantic style and his receding hairline, and at one point put on a Fez, calling William 'the dude'. Harry, famous for his impersonations, then did a high-pitched impression of Kate calling William 'Billy' and of his brother calling Kate 'baby'. He also said that he loved Kate like a sister, and that her relationship with his brother inspires him. One partygoer leaving the Buckingham Palace event in the early hours of Saturday morning told the *Mail on Sunday*: 'Harry said William was the perfect brother. It was exactly how you would expect a best man's speech to be. He cracked loads of jokes about William. He called him a "dude" several times. He kept coming back to it, saying "What a dude"'.

Although Chelsy was his guest at the wedding, it didn't signal another long-term reunion for the couple. After six years, although they couldn't seem to be apart, they unfortunately couldn't seem to be together either. That summer, as Chelsy became involved with property developer Taylor McWilliams, Harry dated willowy blonde lingerie model Florence Brudenell-Bruce. They met through mutual friends and they would meet up at her home in Notting Hill. But she wasn't keen on such a high-profile relationship and after a month or so she eventually returned to her ex-boyfriend, banker Henry St George.

*

Harry was keeping busy. He was based in Stowmarket, a small Suffolk town near his base at RAF Wattisham, and spending time with his cousins and friends. In August he attended Zara Phillips' wedding to England rugby player Mike Tindall, which took place in the Palace of Holyroodhouse in Edinburgh. The night before, the royal party enjoyed a pre-wedding celebration on the Royal Yacht *Britannia* – the place of many memories for all of them, and being together for two joyful family weddings in the space of four months was a cause for celebration.

William and Harry had always been close to Zara and during the service the following day they took turns reading from her favourite childhood book *The Velveteen Rabbit*, before everyone let their hair down afterwards for a party fuelled by Snow Leopard cocktails – a potent combination of amaretto, rum, cream and coffee. The next day, Harry headed back to London on easyJet, and the prince of the people then hit the festival season, going to Womad with his friend Tom Inskip – Skippy – with whom he climbed up onto one of the stages, whereupon the lead singer of punk band Gogol Bordello spilled some red wine on him, and then to Wireless in Hyde Park with Zara, at one point hoisting a little girl onto his shoulders so she had a better view.

During the week he was working, and on his time off, he enjoyed himself in his own inimitable style. At the end of August, he headed to Hvar in Croatia with Skippy. They flew with easyJet but stayed on a yacht moored off the coast. One night they headed to the Veneranda nightclub, which is housed in a renovated sixteenth-century church with a capacity for 1,000 people. Veneranda's marketing manager, Sanja Britt Jusic, said afterwards that Harry was offered the VIP area but wanted to mingle with everyone else. The house music was pumping, and after a few tequilas, the prince joined other revellers in the swimming pool, bounding around, chatting to the other guests and enjoying himself. Jusic said, 'We do not normally let people swim in the pool for safety reasons. But I do not think even security could control him – he is a serious party boy and just wanted to go wild and let his hair down. It was impossible to stop him but when you see someone having such a good time you don't really want to. We just made sure he wasn't getting hurt. He was jumping in and out of the pool all night. I was worried about him slipping and hurting himself or catching a cold, so I gave him one of the T-shirts we sell in our shop. After putting it on, he looked just like a club waiter.'

In September, Harry turned twenty-seven, and before long he was having dinner with Chelsy once again, although their relationship wasn't to be, and when he flew out for helicopter training in San Diego, he was a single man again. He was taking part in Exercise Crimson Eagle, which gives Army Air Corps pilots vital experience in live firing exercises on the vast military ranges in the south-western United States. He was living his 'normal life', exploring San Diego when he could, riding around on his motorbike, and enjoying a brief romance with cocktail waitress, Jessica Donaldson, who worked in the Andaz Hotel in San Diego. It was remarked that, being a brunette and with a large floral tattoo snaking round her torso, Jessica was not Harry's usual type.

The *Sun* reported that he scored top marks in all the challenges he faced at the Naval Air Facility in El Centro, California. An army source quoted by the newspaper said: 'There are many skills needed to be a top-drawer Apache pilot but apparently it's Harry's flying that is particularly impressive. His handling, hand-eye coordination, reaction speeds – he's a natural.'

In February, Harry had completed his sixteen-month training. He was awarded top prize for 'best front-seat pilot', which 'marked out the student whose overall performance during the course is assessed as the best among his peer group'. He was ready to go back to war. It was just a matter of when.

CHAPTER THIRTEEN

The prince, the pop star and the Olympian

Chelsy had been a part of Harry's life for seven years – they had grown up together, from teenagers into young adults. They had been through living thousands of miles apart, break-ups, relationships with other people, boozy antics, globetrotting in different directions, heavy workloads, bad press, the investigation into his mother's death and war. By the end of 2011 she was still in his life as a support and as a friend, and when Harry returned from the US in time for Christmas, Chelsy was at the Henry van Straubenzee Memorial Carol Concert at St Luke's Church in Chelsea, and they greeted each other with a hug. Although they were not in a relationship, they were in the same social group, and still remain good friends.

Rounding off the jubilant royal wedding year, Harry celebrated the month of December with a string of events, partying off-duty with David Beckham at the exclusive members-only Arts Club, where he ended up dancing with comedian and chat-show host

Alan Carr, and then very much on duty accompanying William and Kate to the *Sun* Military Awards. However, just as the family prepared for their traditional celebrations over the festive season – the first that Kate was to attend – Prince Philip was admitted to hospital. Suffering from chest pains, on 23 December he was airlifted to local Papworth Hospital and was found to have a blocked coronary artery. A stent was fitted, which, although deemed a minor procedure, given his age meant that the prince was kept in the hospital over Christmas as a precaution.

The Queen had a full house at Sandringham that year, and although it was thought to be the first time she and her husband had been apart at Christmas, the rest of the family's plans continued much as they normally would. The only difference was that on the afternoon of Christmas Day, Harry drove Beatrice and Eugenie, while William drove Peter and Zara Phillips and they all went to visit their grandfather in hospital. Philip was discharged soon after Christmas, and he returned to his family in Sandringham, although that year he didn't take part in the annual Boxing Day shoot.

After welcoming the new year in so many times in sunny African destinations, now that he and Chelsy had split for good, this time Harry headed to the Swiss ski resort of Verbier with his friends, plus Beatrice and Eugenie. They stayed at the Hotel Nevai – a cool boutique hotel that looks like a traditional alpine lodge from the outside but inside is modern, with sunken seating areas, droplet-shaped lamps, a four-metre long fireplace in the bar and sleek, white minimalist bedrooms. He and Skippy threw snowballs from their balcony and, as the New Year rang in, they drank and danced in the glass-fronted Farinet club, which literally vibrates, before heading over to Guy Pelly's latest offshoot of his club Public, where they spent time in the VIP area called the Sweet Room, which was decked out like a traditional sweet shop.

*

Upon his return, Harry finally completed his training after a gruelling eighteen months, which meant he was now a qualified Apache pilot. To celebrate, he and William took a boys' trip, a shooting weekend in Spain. They stayed on an estate owned by the Duke of Westminster, Gerald Grosvenor – Britain's third-richest man and one of William's godfathers. Situated in the backwaters of rural Cordoba, the area was teeming with wildlife, including stag and boar, and along with a few friends, they stayed in one of three luxurious hunting lodges built at the heart of the estate. The ten-bedroom property has marble floors, its own jacuzzi and sauna, while the estate even has its own petrol station.

It was the Queen's Diamond Jubilee year and while she and Prince Philip stayed in the UK, visiting as many different parts of the country as possible, she left it to the younger members of the family to represent her overseas. So, while Prince Charles, Princess Anne, Prince Andrew and Prince Edward headed to the four corners of the Commonwealth, and William and Kate covered Singapore, Malaysia and the South Pacific, it was decided that Harry would visit the Caribbean.

Harry had been to the Caribbean before (visiting Necker as a young boy with his mother and brother, cruising the West Indies with his family, and holidaying in Barbados with Chelsy), and he had been on overseas royal engagements before (to Africa and Haiti), but until now he had never been given the responsibility or status of embarking on his own royal tour, and it was a big deal for him.

Royal tours are put together to promote strong links between the UK and other countries around the world – for trade, business and good relations. Many places and activities are considered before deciding which would be the best fit with the visiting royal. The tour would usually include an official welcome, where the royal party takes the royal salute from the local military; meeting with prime ministers, governors and overseas royals; paying their respects to those who have died for their country at war; and taking an interest in what is important to that particular country. On a personal level, a visiting royal also likes to include engagements that tie in with the charities they support. It helps if there is something visual about each engagement, something that would look interesting in the newspapers and garner coverage around the world – thus delivering the message, the real reason for the trip in the first place.

On his Caribbean tour, it soon became clear to press and public alike that Harry was not just the joker, the hothead and the headline-maker, he was also now a fully fledged senior member of the royal family. The tour was marked with not one, or two but a slew of key moments for which he will always be remembered. Getty photographer Chris Jackson says, 'Harry's first tour was without a doubt one of the most enjoyable royal trips I have been on. His sense of humour and ability to always amuse with the unexpected made for great photos and a trip that energized the press pack and generated a huge amount of positive coverage back in the UK. There is never any show for the media, you are always seeing the "real" Harry. You never know what to expect.'

First, Harry headed to Belize on the north-eastern coast of Central America, where he started as he meant to go on – self-deprecating and professional, but with a glint in his eye – giving a speech in which he apologized to the Belizeans that they were 'stuck with' him instead of the Queen. He attended a night-time street party, sampling local food and drinks, and named a street in his grandmother's honour. The following day, in the melting 30-degree heat, he visited Mayan ruins, christened a Diamond Jubilee canoe by pouring a bottle of beer over it, and lay a wreath of poppies for British soldiers at Price Barracks in Belize City.

He then flew on to the Bahamas where he met with the Governor-General (the Queen's representative in the Bahamas) and attended a church service, wearing the No. 1 Tropical Dress of the Blues and Royals for the first time.

After a quick change, he then spent a few hours on the idyllic Windermere Island, which was a trip made at his request as it was where Charles and Diana holidayed when Diana was pregnant with William. He then attended a youth rally at the Thomas A. Robinson National Stadium, and laid another wreath at the Royal Bahamas Defence Force memorial.

It was when he set foot on Jamaica that the tour proceeded with a whip-crack speed in a rush of colour – in one day alone covering sports, politics, children, music and dance – with a pop superstar and a world-famous Olympian thrown in for good measure. On a humid day, as clouds laid low over the mountains, Harry arrived at the University of the West Indies sports track, for a running competition with the fastest man who has ever lived – the six-foot-five streak of greased lighting that is Usain Bolt. After chatting for a while, they limbered up for a race, facing each other like boxers and puffing up their chests, before Harry distracted Bolt with the classic 'What's that over there?' tactic, and raced off down the track to cross the finishing line, arms outstretched in an image that was immediately beamed around the world. Afterwards, Bolt said, 'Yeah, man, he cheated. He knew he couldn't beat me but wanted to go back to London saying he did. I've told him I want a rematch at London 2012 but Harry said, "I'm busy".' Harry, however, promised to visit Bolt in the Olympic village, and to watch him race – and he stayed true to his word.

After changing out of his sports kit into a light linen suit, he headed to a local law school to watch a mock murder trial and, outside, girls dissolved into tears at seeing him so close up, while one excitedly exclaimed, 'He asked me if we all have to go back to studies this afternoon, and then he winked at me!'

Then, once again with the words about Diana from his eighteenth birthday interview echoing, he 'finished the things she didn't get the chance to' when he visited Bustamante Children's Hospital. This was an especially poignant visit for Harry, as his mother was scheduled to visit the hospital in 1997, but passed away before she got the chance. With its open-plan layout and buildings painted pink and peppermint green, with all the windows open and flapping with lace curtains, it was a far cry from the state-of-the-art hospitals he had visited in more developed countries. He stayed longer than was scheduled, sitting by children's bedsides and chatting to them, later expressing concern that his visit to the hospital wouldn't be covered in the papers, as it might be overshadowed by his encounter with Usain Bolt from earlier in the day.

He then went for lunch at Devon House, the official residence of the Prime Minister, Portia Simpson-Miller, who had always been in favour of abolishing the Queen as Jamaica's head of state. However, she greeted Harry with a hug, held his hand as they posed for pictures, and gushed afterwards, 'I'm in love with him!'

His incredible day still wasn't over, as Harry's last engagement was to RISE Life Management Services – a facility for inner-city kids who don't have many opportunities, offering education and vocational training. Harry's tie was soon off, and he enjoyed the dancing performances that were put on, before one young girl approached him and led him to dance with her among the other performers. Luckily he was wearing his blue suede shoes ... It was here he also met Bob Marley's widow Rita, who gave him one of her late husband's scarves, striped in the red, green and gold of Jamaica's national colours.

Harry is a big Bob Marley fan, and respectfully kissed the older lady's hands, later quoting the famous reggae star in one of his speeches, 'Her Majesty has asked me to extend her good wishes to you all, and is sorry she can't be here – so you're stuck with me ... but don't worry, cos every little ting gonna be all right!' It was also at RISE Life that Harry had a chat with Gary Barlow, who was visiting the island to source musicians for his Jubilee single 'Sing'. When Barlow discovered Harry was to be there at the same time, he decided to try to enlist the prince for a contribution, and ended up getting Harry to play tambourine on the track.

The pace of Harry's first tour was lively, and the following day he was back in military fatigues for a shooting exercise at Up Park Military Base, cracking the air with ear-splitting shots when he fired several rounds from an M40 rifle into the head and throat of a human silhouette target. He couldn't help a jibe at the press when he gestured towards the targets, 'Anyone with a camera want to stand up that end?'

He then headed to a private island lit up entirely in red, yellow and green for a night of singing and dancing performances alongside local beauty queens. The air was scented with flowers

and coconut oil, and all guests were greeted off the boat by
fire-breathers and stilt-walkers. Harry later wrote a letter to
the Governor General to express his thanks for the country's
hospitality, writing 'Wow! I have totally fallen for Jamaica and
its people. My grandmother, the Queen, was so right about you.
Thank you for showing me such a good time, and allowing me
to visit so many cultural, historical and fun places. The warmth
that I received from the moment I set foot on your awesome
island has been totally overwhelming. In passing on your good
wishes to the Queen for her Diamond Jubilee, I can't wait to tell
her all about my three-day visit. I have made life-long friends
– and cool ones at that! Please can I come back and visit …
lots? Harry'.

*

The Diamond Jubilee part of his trip done, Harry then flew
to Brazil for the fundraising portion – much in the way that
William and Kate had done the previous year when they headed
to LA after their Canadian tour. After a helicopter ride over Rio
de Janeiro, Harry spent his first night in the city at the GREAT
launch, celebrating everything great about Britain. There were
replica red telephone boxes and a miniature Big Ben, while
guests sipped special cocktails created by Claridges Hotel and
ate miniature roast beef and Yorkshire puddings and mini
shepherd's pies. Cutting a dash in a sharp suit, Harry was greeted
on the red carpet by whirling sequinned samba dancers, before
taking a cable car up Sugarloaf Mountain to look around a James
Bond exhibition and view the FA cup and Olympic Torch. All
the lights of Rio were spread below and the famous Christ
the Redeemer statue was illuminated on nearby Corcovado

Mountain under a full moon. One of the local reporters couldn't contain herself and called out, 'Let's marry, Harry!'

The prince then looked round a display of Bentleys and Aston Martins, took in a pop-up fashion show by one of his sister-in-law Kate's favourite designers – Issa, formed by Brazilian-born Daniella Helayel. David Beckham then appeared on a video from LA, apologizing for not being able to be there and introducing Harry with the words, 'He will get the party started as only he can.' Before Harry bantered back, 'That was David Beckham, apparently he used to play football!'

The following day, Harry put his own stamp further on his tour by engaging in sporting activities with children and local athletes. Despite the sizzling 31 degrees on Flamengo Beach, Harry ran the Sport Relief mile in eight minutes, sixty-two seconds, crossing the finishing line in a Prince William mask that someone had given him. After that, under the shadow of Sugarloaf Mountain, he coached local kids in a rugby match, much to their delight, throwing them around and cheating by holding on to their jerseys. He later said, 'The most important thing in life for me is kids. I don't know if I got that from my mum or my father but I just have this massive kid inside me and I have that connection with kids and always will.' He then played volleyball with double world champion Adriana Behar, throwing water over one of his teammates, and slam-dunking a few points.

In the afternoon, he headed into dangerous territory when he ventured into Complexo do Alemão, a *favela* (shanty town) that had been the scene of a week-long shoot-out between police and violent drug dealers just over a year earlier. The army were now overseeing the rehabilitation of the area, but there were still similar problems in nearby areas, and even during Harry's visit there was a shoot-out between gangs and police just a mile away. The colonel in charge of the area revealed, 'As well as bullets, home-made bombs were thrown and we responded with stun grenades.' Once inside the community, it was quite something to experience. There were tin shacks and crumbling buildings with huge holes in the walls, and a foul-smelling river. There were 300 army personnel on duty for Harry's visit, during which he was welcomed by a children's choir, inspected a health clinic, opened a community centre being funded by Sport Relief, and played cricket with local children. One girl said, 'I've been practising a few words in English like I love you', while another added, 'I have never seen anyone so white with so many freckles. Everyone wants to be his princess.'

He wrapped up his triumphant first solo tour playing a polo match to raise funds for Sentebale, drawing whoops from the crowd as he drove a horse-drawn carriage onto the polo field at Haras Larissa. He had shown the kaleidoscopic display of his talents – the things that make up who he is; the three different sides that he often refers to – soldier, man and prince. He showed he could shoot a man in the throat at thirty metres; he melted the resolve of the Prime Minister with his charm; he respectfully kissed the hands of an older lady, and got down on the dance floor with the younger ones; he played rugby with local kids; sat at the bedside of those who were sick; played tambourine on a number one single; and beat the fastest man in the world in a running race. What more was there?

*

In fact his mind was on thoughts of romance and, especially as he was approaching his twenty-eighth birthday and seeing his brother and sister-in-law so happy, he couldn't help but think of matters of the heart. Although his link to Chelsy was ongoing and they remained friends, their relationship was over. Harry had been out in the clubs and bars but he wanted something more, and when he gave an interview to American TV station ABC, he said, 'I've longed for kids since I was very, very young. I'm waiting to find the right person – someone who's willing to take on the job.'

Although many might be shocked that the idea of marrying Harry would be anything other than a delight and an honour, Harry had found that the free-spirited girls he was attracted to were not keen to embark on a life in the royal family. It was a sentiment summed up by actress Anne-Marie Mogg a few years earlier, when one of his friends approached her in a club on Harry's behalf and she declined the invitation to join him. She later told the *Daily Mail*, 'He is a very good-looking guy. He's much taller and stronger-looking than I thought from photographs. If he hadn't been a royal, I probably would have gone over.'

Instead of spending time with a girlfriend, Harry focused on work, friends and family, and also underwent a change of address when, along with William and Kate, he moved into Kensington Palace. The two brothers had spent their childhoods there with their parents and after the divorce they continued to live there with their mother until her death. Neither wanted to return to the apartments in which they grew up, but William and Kate had selected Apartment 1A, which was Princess Margaret's old home. In the ten years following their aunt's death it had been used as office and exhibition space and so extensive renovations were needed to be undertaken before they could move in. In the meantime, they lived in a smaller property in the grounds called Nottingham Cottage. Harry was staying in Prince Charles's former private secretary Sir Michael Peat's old quarters, Apartment 4B, a tiny space with one bedroom, kitchen and sitting room. As soon as the couple moved into their new home then Harry would move into Nottingham Cottage.

In April, Harry headed to Romania with friends, as guests of Transylvanian count Tibor Kalnoky. Prince Charles owns properties in Romania, which are maintained by the Count, and Harry and his friends spent some of their time riding motorcycles through the snowy village of Valea Zalanului.

Shortly after his return Harry was linked to pop-singer Mollie King from The Saturdays, but the flirtation was over before it began. They were out together in the same group a few times, including after-hours karaoke in new London club Bunga-Bunga, but nothing ever came of it.

Soon Harry was showing interest in another well-spoken sylph-like blonde, and that relationship looked like it might have a future ...

CHAPTER FOURTEEN

One crazy summer ...

I f signs were needed that Harry was stepping out of his old party-prince reputation as neatly as yesterday's clothes, it came in early 2012 when he was invited to Washington to be presented with a humanitarian award. In May, he flew over to receive the Atlantic Council's 2012 award for distinguished humanitarian leadership for his charitable work with wounded service members. Dressed in a tuxedo, he humbly accepted the award and dedicated it to those who had been killed or injured in the line of duty, adding that he felt he still hadn't done nearly enough. This was just the beginning of a more statesman-like few months, although, along with the rest of the country, he was celebrating an extraordinary summer.

The following month he was there when his grandmother the Queen celebrated her Diamond Jubilee. Stepping out into the freezing cold, wet grey morning in June, along with William and Kate, he waved to the cheering crowds who had lined the banks of the Thames for the Diamond Jubilee River Pageant, and joined the rest of his family on the royal barge, the *Spirit of Chartwell* for their two-hour journey down to Tower Bridge. It was the first time a river pageant of this scale had been staged for 300 years and his family headed up a procession of 1,000 vessels. Floating orchestras, waterborne fireworks, on-board fountains, half-tonne bells, bagpipes, Bollywood musicians and a Bond film speedboat were all part of the seven-and-a-half-mile-long flotilla, while other vessels contained World War II veterans, paralympians, injured service people, breast cancer survivors, musicians and distinguished guests.

After a very cold and wet journey, the royal family arrived at Tower Bridge, where they watched the rest of the flotilla pass, with the unfinished Shard skyscraper stretching ragged and ghostly into the foggy murk above them. Bells clanged and ship horns blasted as sea shanties were performed that had the royal family jigging, and the whole event ended with canons exploding as a shower of pink and red fireworks poured from London Bridge. Despite the unseasonably cold wind and needling rain, the one million people who lined the riverbanks didn't falter, and neither did the Queen and Prince Philip who were aged 86 and 91 respectively. Although custom-made thrones had been provided for them to take a seat on board the *Spirit of Chartwell*, the pair stood the whole way, paying their respects to those who had turned out to celebrate with them. The next day Prince Philip was admitted to hospital with a bladder infection, but he had done his duty.

In a marked difference to the previous day, the Diamond Jubilee concert took place on a balmy summer evening, and guests were able to bask in the sunshine in the specially erected stands around Buckingham Palace. Gary Barlow had put together the extravaganza, and while the Golden Jubilee concert had taken place in the gardens of Buckingham Palace round the back, he wanted the Diamond Jubilee concert to be more inclusive and so it was held around the front of the palace, staged around the impressive Queen Victoria Memorial, and those without a ticket swelled down the Mall in a surge of waving Union flags. In the electric, expectant atmosphere, Robbie Williams kicked off the proceedings, accompanied by the drummers and trumpeters of the second battalion of the Coldstream Guards, who launched into 'Let Me Entertain You' as he strutted around the bronze lions at the base of the memorial.

An eclectic mix of entertainers took to the stage, and as the sun set, Grace Jones hula-hooped through 'Slave to the Rhythm', and Ed Sheeran strummed out his hit 'The A Team'. It is well known that the Queen is not a fan of pop music and this was more an event for the younger members of the family and her people, so she arrived later, leaving Harry, William, Kate, Beatrice, Eugenie, Peter, Autumn, Zara and Mike to enjoy the concert from the beginning. Since Prince Philip was still in hospital, the Queen arrived alone in time for a rendition of 'Sing', the song written by Gary Barlow and Sir Andrew Lloyd Webber and performed by the Military Wives Choir and a varied collection of musicians whom Barlow had found from all over the Commonwealth, including a tambourine ting from Harry that had been recorded in Jamaica. It was followed by a cracking rendition of the appropriate 'Diamonds Are Forever' from Dame Shirley Bassey.

In the dark of the summer night, the front of Buckingham Palace was projected with rose petals as classical singers Alfie Boe and Renée Fleming sang 'Somewhere' from a Buckingham Place balcony, and a rip-roaring finale saw Elton John's stage lit in fuchsia for 'Your Song', Stevie Wonder's specially amended

'Isn't She Lovely', and Sir Paul McCartney's raucous version of 'Ob-la-di, ob-la-da' with all of the evening's performers on stage and the crowds singing along on their feet. Prince Charles and the Queen made their way to the stage, where the prince paid tribute to his mother, as well as his absent father.

Harry, William and Kate attended the after-party and despite their late night spent mingling with the likes of Kylie Minogue and Will.i.am, they were all bright-eyed and bushy-tailed for the Service of Thanksgiving the next morning at St Paul's Cathedral. The Queen was, once more, unaccompanied as Prince Philip was still in hospital but she was surrounded by Charles, Camilla and many of her children and grandchildren, before they all headed back for a balcony appearance at Buckingham Palace. Usually on such occasions the Queen is flanked by Philip, all of her children, all their children, and her cousins and their offspring, but on this occasion it was a stark yet strong quintet who stood around her. With Charles to one side and William to the other the future of the monarchy looked strong, with the first and second in line to the throne with their wives and Harry.

*

Before the excitement of the Olympics, Harry and William went surfing in Polzeath, Cornwall with their friends Thomas van Straubenzee and Skippy, and Harry also attended the premiere of the latest Batman film *The Dark Knight Rises* in Leicester Square. It was after that that he first stepped out into a very public arena with the girl he had recently been wooing. After stopping by at Freemason's Hall in Covent Garden, they went on separately to London bar Le Salon, and the following day the name Cressida Bonas was sprinkled liberally throughout the newspapers.

Harry and Cressida had been introduced by Princess Eugenie, who is good friends with Cressida. In 2010 they had run the London Marathon together, along with thirty-two other friends, making up a giant caterpillar and entering the Guinness Book of Records for the largest number of people tied together to cross the finishing line. It was after that event that the group of friends, including Richard Branson's children Holly and Sam, as well as Cressida's half-sister Isabella Calthorpe and Princess Beatrice, decided to set up the Big Change, a charitable trust working for young people. In turn, Harry and Cressida had met at the invitation-only Valley Festival, which is hosted every year by Harry's friend Arthur Landon. This year, the festival was held to raise funds for the Big Change, and the theme was 'Out of the Enchanted Woodland'. The willowy twenty-three-year-old Cressida held many similar qualities to the girls Harry had previously been involved with: blonde, pretty and relaxed, with a bohemian streak, however where Chelsy was fiery and earthy, Cressida was airy and otherworldly.

Cressida comes from a sprawling arty, aristocratic family that has flitted around the edges of celebrity for decades. Her mother is sixties cover girl Lady Mary-Gaye Curzon, and her father is businessman Jeffrey Bonas. Jeffrey was her mother's third husband and Cressida grew up the youngest of five stepsiblings. Pandora Cooper-Key, from Mary-Gaye's first marriage, is the eldest and is an accessories designer for Vivienne Westwood. The three Anstruther-Gough-Calthorpes, products of Lady Gaye's second marriage, are artist Georgiana, actress Isabella (who was once the object of Prince William's affections and is now married to their friend Sam Branson) and Jacobi who has played polo with Harry and William. Cressida is also friends with her half-siblings' other half-sibling actress Gabriella Wilde, who is forging a career on the big screen in the remake of *Carrie*, while Cressida's cousin is *Made in Chelsea* star Richard Dinan.

Cressida's parents divorced when she was five, and she then split her time between their country estates, as well as her mother's Chelsea pied-à-terre. Growing up in a creative and free-spirited environment coloured Cressida's choices and as she hit double figures she spent several years at the Royal Ballet School, before enrolling in Prior Park College in Bath on a sports scholarship and then moving onto Stowe, where she took roles in many student plays. She then took a year out as a ski instructor before doing a dance degree at Leeds University. After living in Australia for a while, babysitting and waitressing, she moved back to the UK to study contemporary dance at Trinity Laban Conservatoire of Music and Dance in Greenwich. She and Harry were in the early stages of their romance, and weren't quite girlfriend/boyfriend yet, but they were on their way.

Harry's summer of official duties was far from over, and he had the honour of attending the opening ceremony of the London Olympics, where the world watched in wonder as the green pastures inside the stadium, gave way to towering chimney stacks that rose smoking from the ground, a giant set of Olympic Rings raining fire, a flock of flying Mary Poppins, 320 trampoline beds bouncing with children in striped pyjamas, and luminous winged cyclists. After the spectacle came the games themselves and Harry, William and Kate were regular spectators in their capacity as Olympics ambassadors. They were there to watch the princes' cousin Zara in the cross-country eventing competition, which helped her team win silver, as well as the artistic gymnastics men's team final where Team GB won bronze. Harry was also with William at Eton Dorney as the women's pair Heather Stanning and Helen Glover won Team GB's first gold medal of the games, and they also went to the Olympic village and met athletes including Super Saturday star Jessica Ennis.

Harry was also in the velodrome with William and Kate, Princess Anne and her husband Timothy Laurence, Sophie, Countess of Wessex and Prime Minister David Cameron to watch Sir Chris Hoy race to victory and then, true to the promise he had made earlier in the year, he was with William and Kate to witness Usain Bolt sprint to victory in the 100 metres – wearing Bob Marley's red, green and gold striped scarf that Rita Marley had given to him in Jamaica. He was also very present behind the scenes, and was joined by Culture Secretary Jeremy Hunt at Clarence House at a reception for twenty-five young medal-winners from the first School Games that had been held at the Olympic Park earlier in the year. Urging them to think about the Rio Games in 2016, and taking a playful pop at Hunt who had earlier broken a bell while ringing it, he said, 'I urge you to pick up the torch – or in Jeremy's case the bell – and I expect to see your faces again when you stand on the podium at Rio and beyond.' He then chatted to the young athletes and their families.

He was also interviewed, alongside William, by Sue Barker for the BBC in the Olympic Park and, with Kate, he visited the Olympic Village to meet Sophie Hosking, the gold medal-winning rower. Then it was all eyes on him as he represented his family in the closing ceremony. This was a very significant and important moment for him. The Queen and Prince Philip were taking their annual trip to Balmoral and enjoying a break from the Jubilee and Olympics excitement, while William was on duty as a search and rescue pilot. Harry was accompanied once more by Kate and they basked in the glow of the closing ceremony, with a lit-up miniature London, choirs singing

'Imagine' as an illuminated ultraviolet profile of John Lennon rose from the ground, the Spice Girls surfing on black cabs, Russell Brand on a bus that turned into an octopus, and Eric Idle as a human cannonball singing 'Always Look on the Bright Side of Life' surrounded by rollerskating nuns.

As the glorious summer came to a close, Harry knew that he was off to war again in just a few weeks and took a two-pronged sunshine holiday with a group of friends to make the most of his final days of freedom. First, he headed to Necker in the Caribbean, where he had first visited as a child. He was now good friends with Virgin boss Richard Branson's children Sam and Holly Branson, and Sam played host to a group of their mutual friends there to celebrate his twenty-seventh birthday at the end of August. Among the group was Sam's fiancée, Isabella Calthorpe, and her half-sister Cressida. Harry's good friend Arthur Landon went fully prepared, taking eight fancy-dress costumes, including a gas mask and Captain Britannia and Storm Trooper costumes, while Cressida donned an electric pink wig and day-glo body paint along with her bikini.

Following the tropical break, some of the party then peeled off and headed home, while Harry and some of his male friends, including Skippy and Arthur Landon, headed off for a boys' holiday to Las Vegas. It was not Harry's first trip to Sin City, as he had visited the previous year, but it was certainly to be his last – for a while at least. As before, he stayed in one of the newer luxury hotels, the Wynn Encore, where he and his party had booked out the Tower Suite, with its own private lift, butler service, chandeliers, a wet bar, mohair-padded walls designed to absorb sound, a massage table and a pool table. The group lived it up – according to the tradition of the neon city – enjoying steak dinners and Jäger Bombs, partying at the hotel's Surrender nightclub, which is set around a pool and rife with bikini-clad go-go dancers. They also played the dice game craps at the hotel's casino.

On one night at the XS nightclub, Harry's group hooked up with a hen party and the prince requested one of their hen night T-shirts. That night he also challenged Olympic swimmer Ryan Lochte to a swimming race. The gold medal winner had been drinking nearby and Harry, spurred on by his successful cheating tactics earlier in the year against Usain Bolt, asked a couple of British holidaymakers to hold Lochte's legs, while he, Harry, once again triumphed against an Olympian. One of the Brits, Adam Aley, later tweeted, 'Just spent my night with Prince Harry and Ryan Lochte ... Life doesn't get any f****g better!!!!!' While his friend Tom Sims tweeted, 'I can't describe how this night was with Harry!! I thru him in the pool.'

But the fun didn't end there. Harry and his friends invited a number of women to continue partying in their suite. British-born Carrie Reichert told the *People* that one of Harry's friends approached her, and she was swept up along with nine other girls to go to the suite to carry on the party. He was, she said, already naked, playing air guitar with pool sticks when she arrived, and she recalled that he shouted out, 'Somebody get me a glove! I'm gonna do a Michael Jackson impression.'

Days later, pictures emerged online of Harry with no clothes on after a game of strip billiards, and hugging a naked female party-goer. He could be identified by the leather string necklace that had been given to him by a Botswana shaman to ward off evil spirits ... although it had proved useless when it came to the camera-phone wielding party-girls who had been consuming them ...

CHAPTER FIFTEEN

Love and war

The fallout was instant, but opinion was varied. Some thought 'good on him – he's young, single and enjoying his life. He hasn't hurt anyone so who cares?' Others believed that as a senior member of the royal family who had been representing the Queen at formal events, he should be more careful about the company he keeps. Harry later said of the incident in an interview with CNN, 'I probably let myself down, I let my family down and I let other people down. It was probably a classic example of me being too much army and not enough prince … but at the end of the day I was in a private area and there should be a certain amount of privacy that one should expect.'

His former protection officer Ken Wharfe, however, believes that the issue is one of security, explaining, 'It would appear there was a breakdown between him and his protection team. Someone has to stand up and say, "If you're going to do this, Sir, I'm going to suggest we keep all the phones in here. No cameras, let's just do a few checks." For some reason Harry thought it would be fine not to.'

It appears the problem was perhaps not the fact that Harry did what he did – that is a part of his character and what makes him the person he is – but more that the pictures were allowed to be taken in the first place. It seems he should have been better protected.

'These circumstances could have been avoided, without denying him the fun,' says Wharfe. 'He is a member of the royal family. He's a highly known global figure. He, his brother and Kate are probably the three most famous people in the world. As a security advisor, you are, in my view, permitted to give advice when you see things going wrong. You have a moral responsibility. The relationship between Harry and his protection team is not what it should be, and that's the problem. The pictures being taken was preventable.'

Shortly after his return from Vegas, Harry attended the WellChild Awards, which celebrates the bravery of some of the UK's most seriously ill children and the dedication of the people who get involved with the charity. WellChild had been set up in 1977 and was called 'Kidney' to begin with, as it set out to fund research into kidney disease. However, as the charity strengthened and grew, it broadened out its beneficiaries to include all children affected by life-threatening and life-limiting conditions in the UK, and was renamed 'WellChild' in 2003. The charity contacted Harry three years after it started up, introducing their work and their aims, to see if he would consider becoming their patron. There was delight all round when the patronage was confirmed in 2007.

The first time Harry met some of the children was at the Concert for Diana later that year when a group of children and their families were invited to meet William and Harry backstage. 'It is hugely important to have Prince Harry as our patron,' says WellChild CEO Colin Dyer. 'The impact really can't be underestimated. His involvement and support have helped give many children, young people and families some experiences they wouldn't otherwise have had.'

Over his years as patron Harry has been more than just a high-profile figurehead helping to draw attention to the charity. To help him better understand what the children and their families go through, as well as see how the WellChild nurses work with them, he has secretly visited seriously ill children in their homes. 'Visiting them in their own homes helps him better understand the challenges faced by them and their families every day,' says Colin Dyer. 'It has allowed him to talk privately with that child, their family and the nurse, and therefore understand some of the challenges faced by those caring for a seriously ill child, as well as the support WellChild provides.'

Dyer also noted how natural Harry is with children, saying that he treats the children and their families 'with empathy, respect and genuine interest'. When Harry became patron of the charity he was in his early twenties, and now as he approaches his thirtieth birthday Colin Dyer believes that Harry has matured into his role, adding: 'Over the years his understanding of the work and aims of the charity, and the situations faced by the families have developed.'

At the awards ceremony, six-year-old Alex Logan, who had been diagnosed with leukaemia at the age of three, vowed on TV that he would say 'I'm glad you've got your clothes on Prince Harry!' But when they met, Harry pre-empted him with a grin, 'You keep looking up at your mum. It looks like you're dying to say something but you're worried she'll tell you off. I heard you were on ITV earlier and you said something cheeky – but let's not talk about that here.' Alex instead tickled Harry with his toy penguin.

*

Then it was time for Harry to get back into his desert fatigues for his second flight to Afghanistan. On his first tour in 2007, he was not long out of his teens, holding the most junior position of second lieutenant; now in 2012 he was a grown man and a captain. He would also be undertaking a different duty, as co-pilot gunner of an Apache attack helicopter. Apart from being known as 'flying guns', Apaches are also known to the Brits as 'call sign ugly', and Harry has said, 'I don't know where "ugly" came from but it's a pretty ugly beast and I think it's very cool.' The pilot sits in the back, and the co-pilot gunner is up front and in charge. During his course, Harry had started out in the back flying the Apache but he was so good that he was bumped up to the front. His abilities were recognized by his Commanding Officer in Afghanistan, Lieutenant Colonel Tom De La Rue, who stated: 'He was awarded the best co-pilot gunner award on that course and that was absolutely the right decision that was made. He's been performing superbly out here. He really is on top of his game. He's an excellent co-pilot gunner.'

Harry and his pilot were to be providing a range of services, including giving cover for the emergency helicopters that transport injured troops from the battlefield to the hospital, and providing protection to troops operating on the ground who were clearing compounds and villages thought to be bases for the Taliban. Basically if there were people on the ground who were vulnerable, Harry would be flying to their rescue. He later said, 'Our job out here is to make sure the guys are safe on the ground. If that means shooting someone who's shooting them, then we'll do it.' They were comments that were criticized as incendiary by some. However, it was a part of his job, and given that he was manning a gun, it was obvious what he would be doing with it.

On 7 September, just days before his twenty-eighth birthday, Harry flew out from Brize Norton with hundreds of other military personnel. On his earlier tour, he had been stationed in a few different remote and isolated bases around the country, with just a few handfuls of men, and he was often in the thick of the action. This time, with his different role, he was based for the duration of his four-and-a-half-month deployment in Camp Bastion in Helmand Province – the biggest military base in the country. It wasn't the only difference. Instead of the media knowing about the deployment and having to keep silent about it until his return, this time everyone knew he was going. He would have preferred to be on the ground with his regiment, but it was safer for him to be in the air. No Apache pilot has been killed since the start of the war. 'The thinking is that being an Apache pilot is quite an anonymous job and the Apache is already a target,' Harry said. 'They can't be more of a target than they already are.'

At twenty-seven square miles, the sprawling Camp Bastion is the largest British overseas military base built since World War II and is home to 30,000 military personnel. Surrounded by blast walls, with watch towers manned by heavily-armed soldiers and chain link fences topped with rolls of razor wire, there are radar cameras and motion monitors around the perimeter that can sense any movement. There is a sign saying 'No filming or cameras permitted', although someone has stencilled a Banksy style rat holding a camera next to the lettering. Once again, Press Association photographer John Stillwell flew over to capture images of Harry at work, and he explained, 'Camp Bastion is the sort of place where you could get lost because it all looks the same. Everything is sandy and dusty and everything's made from Hesco, a wire mesh that comes in flat-packs, and you open it up into a big square and fill it up with sand and rubble and that becomes your wall.' There are also murals all over the base dedicated to the men who have served there.

Just a week after Harry's arrival, on the eve of his twenty-eighth birthday, there was an attack on the camp as the Taliban targeted him for an assassination attempt. Under cover of darkness, members of the Taliban dressed in US army uniforms broke into the camp and destroyed six US Harrier jets. A four-hour firefight began, which left two American Marines and eighteen Taliban dead. Harry was a mile away at the time, but speculation that he was given any special treatment was dismissed by the MOD, who stated, 'Claims that Captain Wales was rushed to a "safe house" during the insurgent attack on Camp Bastion are simply not true ... he was treated much the same as any service member deployed to Camp Bastion.' The camp had always been seen as impenetrable and the grave proof that it wasn't was addressed with reviewed security measures, while the rest of the base got on with their work.

Harry got stuck into the routine that would be his life for the next four-and-a-half-months. Along with the other three men on his team, Harry worked shifts of twelve hours on duty, twelve hours off for the duration of his deployment. Although he was in the sprawling Camp Bastion, his small group of four suited him, and they became close friends. They had to be ready to 'scramble' at a moment's notice. A call on the 'shout phone' meant the four would run to the Apache and get in the air as quickly as possible. Harry explained, 'One minute you're asleep, and six-and-a-half minutes later you're speaking to someone on the ground who's being shot at … We all run to the aircraft, at which point you have that taste of blood in your mouth. Six-and-a-half/seven minutes is I think the quickest we have got it going.'

The team would then need to slow down the adrenaline so they could think properly. They couldn't lift off until certain checks were made, including ensuring that no missiles are unlatched. They kept their helmets in the aircraft and would put them on last – the men were allowed to customize their helmets with badges, and Harry's had his American wings on there, 'go ugly early' and 'Pedro'.

After taking off in a vast cloud of choking orange sand, they would rise to around 2,000 feet before they would start getting information back about what was going on. The majority of missions were medical emergencies, rescuing soldiers who had been injured in the field, or accompanying the mobile hospital, with Harry's Apache flying above the mobile hospital to provide cover. He explained, 'Our job is to make sure the Chinook gets in and out safely. Out there it's flat as a pancake. Every compound looks the same and obviously we've got tools to help us pinpoint the physicians. It's less stressful being up here than it is down there. We don't have to put on all the kit and walk through the desert sweating our balls off.'

Every time he left the base he was flying straight into a war zone. There was no special protection – he was as vulnerable as everyone else. The speed at which they could get in the air and to where they were going was key, as once an injury was sustained it was imperative to get the victim to hospital as soon as possible. The 'Golden Hour' is the first hour after injury – how it is treated in that time can make all the difference in saving lives and limbs. In many cases, the timeframe is even less.

Harry controlled the 30-millimetre canon underneath the aircraft, using a helmet-mounted display so that the gun moved to wherever he turned his head. On either side of the Apache are hellfire missiles and rockets. 'If there's people trying to do bad stuff to our guys, we'll take them out of the game.' Harry explained. 'We fire when we have to. Take a life to save a life … When you fire, you get the cordite smell. The whole floor vibrates. When you fire a missile, the whole aircraft shudders a little bit.'

Most of the calls came late at night or first thing in the morning and Harry explained that the worst were at 2.00 or 3.00 a.m. because they would get back at 5 a.m. and there would be no point in going back to sleep. Missions can last up to three hours, which means even in a war zone there are mundanities to be dealt with, especially when the men could be in the air for two or three hours. 'We have travel johns, which are basically piss bags,' explained Harry. 'If I can hold on I will, but once you've been out here for two or three weeks you master the art of peeing sitting down.' The liquid in a travel john crystallizes so there are very few spillages, although Harry said it was tricky when his co-pilot would start swerving the helicopter in order to put him off.

When on duty, there was a lot of time to kill. While the men were waiting for a call they would be situated in the Very High Readiness block, a large tented apartment with lino on the floor in which the four-man crew slept, ate and relaxed as they waited. A large Union flag was pinned to the wall, and all the furniture was makeshift and cobbled together: tables were made from empty ammunition boxes, they sat on battered leatherette sofas that had burst apart and were stuck back together with gaffer tape, and shell cases were used as ashtrays. The 'table' was covered with a red-and-white gingham plastic cloth that they took from the mess, which, according to Harry, looked 'like a picnic table'. There was a large flat-screen TV linked up to a PlayStation, and a bookshelf unit filled with games such as Scrabble, Monopoly and chess, poker chips, and DVDs, including war films *Platoon*, *Full Metal Jacket* and *Black Hawk Down,* comedies *Borat*, *Hot Fuzz* and *Elf*, and classic action films *Bad Boys* and *Con Air*.

They would play 'Uckers', a board game similar to Ludo, which is particular to the military. They played first thing in the morning and whoever lost was 'brew bitch' for the day and would have to make the drinks. Whoever lost the video game FIFA would also be 'brew bitch'. According to Harry, he was the second best of the four at FIFA. The men slept in single beds with a sleeping bag and a duvet – no sheets – and food was in plentiful supply. The storeroom was full of multipacks of everything from instant coffee and bottled water to snacks. They would trade Kit Kats and Nutri-grain bars for fresh coffee and M&Ms with the American service people, and Harry revealed, 'I hate peanut butter. [Rice Krispie] Squares are good. Trackers – I never used to eat them – I do now. Kit Kats and Mars Bars – everybody tries not to eat them but everybody does.'

The men would eat off disposable plates with plastic cutlery, and in a comment that would make his environmentally conscious father proud, Harry said, 'I keep getting upset with people, saying don't use more than one plastic plate unless you have to. Nobody seems to get it. Save the planet and all that.' There were also shops on the base where they could stock up on certain supplies. One small supermarket on the British side sold gym clothes, toiletries, books, DVDs, sleeping bags and pillows, sweets and cigarettes. Meanwhile the bigger American store sold electrical goods, so they could splash out on stereos, iPods and laptops if they felt the need.

When the men were not on duty, they slept in Portakabins stacked on top of each other. Each cabin was split in two, so they shared with one other person, and a few personal affects were allowed. This is where Harry kept a couple of rugs – one from home, the other an Afghan one that someone had given him. In order to ensure rest when they were not on duty, there was silence from 11 p.m. to 6 a.m. The bathrooms contained stainless steel showers, toilets and sinks with metal surfaces that looked like kitchen draining boards. A number of wing mirrors were screwed into the wall to use for shaving mirrors, and there was a rubber grille over the floor for drainage. The personnel would all eat in the cookhouse or mess – a vast room with a canteen and rows and rows of tables covered in red-and-white checked plastic cloths. Soldiers would bring their rifles and leave them under the table, while officers like Harry just carried their 900mm Sig Sauer pistols. They washed their hands before dinner, and wiped the plastic tablecloth afterwards with anti-bacterial wipes – the last thing they needed was a stomach-bug whipping through the base. Breakfast consisted of bacon, sausage, egg and fried bread, and there were usually five or six dinner options. Fruit and veg were available but were often not of the best quality after the flight out.

When he wasn't stationed in the Very High Readiness tent, Harry would eat in the cookhouse and it would be full of hundreds of others. Harry explained, 'I go into the cookhouse and everyone has a good old gawp and that's one thing I dislike about being there, because there's plenty of guys in there who've never met me and therefore look at me as Prince Harry and not as Captain Wales. Which is frustrating and another reason why I would like to be in one of the [smaller bases] and away from it all.'

John Stillwell recalls, 'He really doesn't like being looked at. There were maybe 500–600 people in there and you go in there for breakfast, lunch and supper, and everyone is in camouflage gear so it's really hard to pick someone out. But even then he would always go in just before they finished serving so it would be quieter, and he would always sit somewhere where he couldn't easily be seen. When I suggested doing pictures in there he said, "Do I have to? Everyone will be gawping."'

When the men weren't on duty there were a few ways to pass the time as there were gyms and social clubs on the base, and even a coffee shop and a Pizza Hut. John Stillwell says, 'He'd obviously been working out. I said, "You've been pumping up" and he said, "No, I only go on the bike." He looked like a grown-up man, though, compared to the first time, his shoulders seemed broader. In Afghanistan all these guys do is go to the gym. He looked like he'd been doing weights. He seemed more mature this time round as well.'

Just before Christmas Harry discovered he was going to be an uncle, and became even more protective of his sister-in-law. After twenty-eight years he was no longer to be 'the spare', no longer the third in line to the throne, and to some extent the pressure was off him. However, this is not something that even crossed his mind at this point in his 'man-prince-army' way of thinking.

Over the festive season Camp Bastion was decorated with little plastic Christmas trees with multi-coloured lights and cheap glittery foils hung from the ceiling. Sixty cooks prepared 200 turkeys, 140 joints of beef and 40 boxes of sprouts, while

Harry received honey from Highgrove and Cuban cigars as a gift from Prince Charles. It's traditional for the men to dress in drag at Christmas, but Harry made a more subtle nod by wearing a Father Christmas hat with white pigtails attached.

While he was stationed in Afghanistan, he was also working on the designs for a Sentebale garden for the following year's Chelsea Flower Show. He was very involved with the design and spoke to garden designer Jinny Blom several times when he was away. So in the most unlikely of locations – a war zone in the middle of an unforgiving desert – he pored over designs for an oasis of leafy green calm, planted with forget-me-nots in memory of his mother. He also emailed Sentebale chief executive Cathy Ferrier every two weeks so that he was up-to-date with how everything was going with his charity. Ferrier had taken on the position in 2012, when the charity had been running for six years, and says, 'I was surprised about how hands-on he is. Quite often he'll say, "I'd like to see the plans early on so I can have an input." I'll send him proposals and different things that we're thinking of and he usually makes a couple of comments on everything I send. He usually has a point of view as to whether he wants more of something or less of something or a different idea completely. So he has a lot of input in the early part of planning for all sorts of things that we do. We sent very detailed designs out to him of the layout of the garden.'

Harry also wrote letters home, although perhaps not as often as family members would have liked. In a Christmas massage to the armed forces, Prince Charles revealed that he had received a 'very rare and precious letter' from his son.

It wasn't long, however, before Harry was heading home. There would have been a lot going through his mind as he flew back home, stopping first at Akrotiri in Cyprus – a British

Military base at which all those heading home from war spend a few days to acclimatise. There, they are given a four pack of lager, and can watch comedies and 'decompress'. Harry told *Sky News*, 'I don't know what normal is anymore and never really have done. There's nothing normal about what we've been doing for the last four-and-a-half months. On the last day that I was there a seven-year-old girl got shot down by insurgents. Normality is a very ambiguous thing. I will continue being myself. I will enjoy being a soldier.'

He returned to the UK on 23 January and, after catching up with his immediate family, he went on a skiing holiday to Verbier with Cressida, Prince Andrew, Sarah, Duchess of York, and their daughters Beatrice and Eugenie. While they were there they celebrated Andrew's fifty-third birthday, and it was also notable as it was the first time Harry had been seen in public with Sarah since he was a little boy. He openly kissed his girlfriend as she sat on his knee, and the royal party celebrated with champagne cocktails in the Pot Luck Club in the Farinet Hotel before the younger members of the group moved on to a basement club.

Days later he headed to Lesotho to see how Sentebale's work was going. In the seven years since the charity was set up, camps and networks had been established that help hundreds of children every year with education, life-skills and support. 'You can see the difference with the children who have been to camp,' says Cathy Ferrier. 'They are much more confident and much more knowledgable about the fact they're living with a virus, and that they can live healthily if they adhere to their medication.'

The camps were named Mamohato Camps after Prince Seeiso's mother, and Prince Seeiso explains, 'The message in Lesotho used to be that having HIV was almost like a death sentence. Now we are saying to the children of Lesotho, know your status, be honest and open about your status, there is medication to keep you healthy for longer and support there to help you lead happy and healthy lives. We are saying to them that you have a friend in Sentebale. When you are at the Mamohato Camp, we can nurture you, and with your positive attitude, you can go out igniting the energy within your own peer groups which will also overflow into the community.'

Sentebale also work on education sponsorship programmes, while the herd boys are now reached through night schools that teach basic numeracy and literacy, as well as providing food, protective clothing and counselling to the young boys up in the mountains. Harry visited the Kananelo Centre for the Deaf and St Bernadette's Centre for the Blind, both of which are supported by Sentebale, and the children there were excited to see him.

'Everywhere I go when I'm out there children ask, "Where's Harry? When's Harry coming?"' says Cathy Ferrier. 'I think it's because they know how much he's trying to help. He's always been pretty hands-on. In the first few years he went out there, he was literally painting walls and moving furniture. They've known him for a while and they know through the people in the community centres that he's been helping.' The children's affection for him goes deeper than that, as his affinity with them also draws them to him. 'He has a very natural way with children,' Ferrier continues. 'He's very relaxed and very open. He immediately goes down onto their level, and just seems to brighten them up. It would be good to be able to bottle what he has actually! Quite often when I'm with him he will go off to do something because he's seen a child that he wants to go and talk to. When we went to St Bernadette's there was the usual official party and you direct Harry over where he's supposed to stand and the children were all in a huge long line. He just broke away from the people he was supposed to be walking with and went to the very front of the line. Because they were visually impaired he immediately got hold of their hands, and he said something to every single child – that was not planned and arguably it would have been very easy to say that's going to take too long, but he didn't miss a single one.'

He also met up with a little girl whom he remembered meeting on one of his first trips to the country when her mother was dying. 'When they first met, it was just a couple of days before her mother died,' explains Cathy Ferrier. 'This time they had a very nice chat and she was telling him all about what she had been up to in the last few years.' Harry also met with many of the Sentebale staff who are based in Lesotho and travelled the country seeing the charity's work on the ground. 'The press only see a tiny bit of the trip,' Ferrier explains. 'There are several days when he visits various projects with no press coverage. It's easier for him to see the work when there's no one else around. He went in to see the team and one of the ladies there is affectionately known as "Ma". She's an older lady who's been with us since the beginning, and he gave her the most huge hug when he went in. He's very at home there and he doesn't hold back.'

Harry then flew to Johannesburg for the first Sentebale Gala Dinner to help raise £2.4 million to build the first permanent centre for children and young people infected with, or affected by, HIV and Aids in Lesotho. The Mamohato Centre will provide psychological care and mentoring for children who are often stigmatized as a result of the disease. At the event, Harry gave a speech: 'It seems only right that it should be named after His Majesty and Prince Seeiso's mother, Queen Mamohato Bereng Seeiso. She was so loved as the Mother of the Nation. I hope she would be proud of what we are trying to achieve in her name. I hope that my mother will be proud, too. Maybe they are together somewhere up there, with blueprints and sketches already mapped out! I can only hope we put the swings in the right place.'

Africa continues to be a very special place to Harry, as witnessed by Chris Jackson, royal photographer for Getty Images picture agency. He has been taking pictures of the royal family for over a decade, and has forged a close relationship with Harry. On this particular trip, Jackson took photos of the people of Lesotho and the work Sentebale had been undertaking, which later made up a special London-based exhibition called 'Stories of Hope'. 'Life for Prince Harry can be very structured back in the UK,' says Jackson. 'Formal royal duties and his helicopter job mean that there is always a level of expectancy and structure in his life. From the time I've spent with him in Africa I can see it is somewhere where he truly feels at home. The slow pace of life there, and lack of paparazzi, means that Harry can really enjoy himself in a way that's simply not possible in the UK. It's obvious that Harry feels most at home in a pair of desert boots and khaki trousers in a continent that provides the mix of adventure and anonymity that he and William both crave.'

Jackson explained how important the continent and Sentebale are to the prince. 'Having spent time with both of the princes in Africa, I can see how they both feel at home. It is no coincidence that both their charities work on this continent – with William's charity Tusk Trust working on preventing poaching across the region and Harry with Sentebale. Harry is incredibly passionate about his work with Sentebale – his dedication to the charity is real and from what I've seen none of it is for the media. It's a very personal battle to try and make life better for the people of Lesotho. He interacts with the children with a sensitivity reminiscent of his mother.'

Meanwhile, Prince Seeiso adds, 'Prince Harry has said a number of times that his heart lies in Africa and I think this is evident in the passion he shows not only for Sentebale, but the other causes he supports in Africa. When I first met him, I could see that he felt very relaxed in Africa and it is definitely a place where he can focus on his passions in life and leave behind lots of the attention he receives back in the UK.'

*

Harry flew back to the UK to resume his military duties at RAF Wattisham in Suffolk after his period of leave, meaning he had had to turn down an invitation to join his new girlfriend, Cressida, at her half-sister's wedding to Sam Branson in South Africa just a few days later. However, he was by her side when Isabella and Sam held a wedding party at Isabella's family home in Hampshire for those friends and family who couldn't make it out for the African extravaganza.

With the imminent birth of William and Kate's baby, and with the Queen and Prince Philip now in their late eighties– early nineties, Harry made it clear that he was happy to take on more royal duties. He awarded medals at the London Marathon, and although following the Boston Marathon bombings less than a week earlier, there was speculation as to whether Harry would still attend, he stated in a BBC interview at the London finishing line, 'It was never an option as far as I was concerned. Everyone who was planning on coming is still here – no one has changed any plans.'

He also visited the Warner Bros studios in Leavesden, just outside London, with William and Kate, to launch the Harry

Potter tour, and attended the launch of Walking With The Wounded's South Pole Allied Challenge, where he announced he would be walking with the UK Team later in the year. Last time when a group headed to the North Pole, Harry could only be there for part of it and, in the same way as on his first tour of duty in Afghanistan, he was frustrated that he couldn't be there to support the men he had bonded with in these extreme conditions. This time he would be able to be there for the whole thing. 'Afghanistan will become old news, it's barely on the news now so imagine what it's going to be like in two, three, four, five years' time. Afghanistan will be forgotten to a certain extent and these guys will be forgotten. But with Walking With The Wounded, Help for Heroes, etcetera, we're here to make sure that doesn't happen.' It was also announced that for the first time, those who had sustained mental injuries as well as physical would be a part of the expedition.

Harry then embarked on his second royal tour, and his dedication to wounded service people was one of the focuses of the trip. When he had been in Washington the previous year to receive his humanitarian award, Harry learned of a US event called the Warrior Games, which was like a paralympics for wounded service people. He was immediately fascinated and eager to know more about it with the view to possibly holding a Warrior Games in the UK. And so his US tour was built around him attending the 2013 Games. In May he flew first to Washington, where he had the ladies of Capitol Hill turning out in their droves for a glimpse when he opened an exhibition to promote the work of anti-landmine charity Halo. His mother had been patron of the charity, and he had just become patron of the trust's twenty-fifth anniversary appeal. He was greeted by the First Lady Michelle Obama as he attended an evening reception at the White House for military mothers and their children, and laid wreaths at Arlington National Cemetery.

He then flew to Colorado – with its wide open spaces, fresh Rocky Mountain air and huge skies – for the launch of the Warrior Games. He wore his military fatigues and stood proudly among the other army men. He then started the hand-bike race on a baking hot day and played seated volleyball. When he was interviewed in front of the crowds and asked if he would consider moving to the States, amid the screams of the girls attending, he laughed and said that they wouldn't always be able to guarantee the good weather.

He also enjoyed an informal evening with members of the Help for Heroes team from the UK. 'They all "get" Harry,' says Help for Heroes founder and CEO Bryn Parry. 'Even with what happened in Las Vegas – all the blokes thought that was great, and there was a lot of teasing about that. He met everyone and all he wants to do is talk to them, and they bring out their mobile phones and show him horrific photographs of their wounds and then he's very much one of the guys, and he's pretending he's shocked and the next minute they're all falling around laughing.'

Harry then headed to New Jersey to view the damage done by Hurricane Sandy, before visiting a kids' baseball diamond in Harlem. He was there to promote a partnership between the Royal Foundation's Coach Core initiative, which aims to train up the next generation of sports coaches in the UK, and Harlem RBI's Project Coach, which does much the same thing in that area of New York. Harry loved mixing with the children there – getting down to their level and talking straight with them. He teased them to bring them out of their shells, and mimicked one sassy little girl who pranced away from him. Another, Jolita Brettler, was enamoured, saying, 'He seemed very kind and loving. If he came again I would be right here waiting for him.'

The day after he got back from the tour, Harry visited the Sentebale B&Q garden at the Chelsea Flower Show unannounced, to see it ahead of the official opening the following week, and impressed those nearby with his interest in their gardens. Two days later he proudly showed the Sentebale garden to the Queen and Duke of Edinburgh, as well as Charles, Camilla, Beatrice and Eugenie. The overall effect was a tranquil space with willows and a large central stone floating in a lake of moss, surrounded by forget-me-not meadows. The stone was patterned with hearts and crowns symbolizing the Prince and the loss of his mother, as well as the children in Lesotho who have lost their own parents. The designer, Jinny Blom, had previously worked with Prince Charles on his Chelsea Flower Show garden in 2002.

The *Daily Mail* reported that Charles looked on proudly at his son's efforts and told him, 'This is the great garden is it, after all that effort? I was wondering if it didn't exist.' Harry couldn't resist jesting with his father, 'If there is anything here which might catch your eye we could probably come to a deal. You can't have it, but we can come to a deal.' 'A deal?!' said Charles with mock outrage. It was only then that Harry noticed his grandfather, Prince Philip, waiting to come in. 'Look they're even queuing,' he joked.

When Charles failed to notice Prince Philip, Harry ribbed him: 'Err, Pa, meet your father!', prompting Charles to look up with an exclamation of surprise, before Harry continued, 'You were meant to be looking at strimmers and tractors, Grandpa, I didn't know you were coming. Fantastic!' Harry even teased Philip that the stone centrepiece could be used as a dance-floor, 'Really?' Philip enquired earnestly. 'No, Grandpa, they wouldn't let us,' Harry replied, straight-faced.

Harry and William also visited a new Help for Heroes recovery centre, Tedworth House in Tidworth, Wiltshire. It was one of four centres that opened simultaneously, to offer help and support to fifty residents and fifty day-visitors in each location. Many injured service people returning from war spend months in intensive care, and what follows is a long and painful journey as they learn to live in the world again, coping with the pain, the changes, and the emotional and mental damage that they face. The two brothers were thrilled that the new centres would be able to help them.

Harry also continued his dedicated support for injured service people when he attended the Walking With The Wounded Crystal Ball gala dinner soon afterwards, where he gave a speech explaining, 'For every life taken, which is about 450 in Afghanistan, about 4,000 are injured and that's what we don't hear about. Arms, legs that will never grow back, as well as mental injuries. The image of your best friend being blown up next to you, that's something that will never leave you.' The recovery and care of the military wounded is a very personal cause for Harry and will continue to help shape his royal role in the future.

CHAPTER SIXTEEN

A new hope

As Andy Murray stormed to victory at Wimbledon and speculation about the birth of the new royal baby reached fever pitch, in the summer of 2013 the people of Britain basked in a heat wave. All but a very select group, that is. From 1 July, press pens were erected in front of St Mary's Hospital, Paddington, where both Harry and William had been delivered. It was where the Duchess of Cambridge was due to give birth, and taxi parking bays outside the hospital were suspended for the month of July when the newest member of the royal family was due to be born. As soon as the pens went up, photographers, news crews and reporters started milling, some travelling from across the world, and setting up camp in the soaring temperatures. They waited. And waited.

Finally, over three long weeks later, on Monday 22 July, Kate was admitted to the hospital at around 5.30 a.m. in the early stages of labour. Prince George was born eleven hours later at

4.24 p.m., and both William and Kate spent their first night as parents at the hospital. The new family left St Mary's twenty-four hours later, and Harry met the new addition when he was just over a day old and enjoyed a cuddle with his nephew, before the Cambridges immediately headed to Berkshire to spend the next few weeks with Kate's family while William was on paternity leave.

Two days later Harry attended Sentebale's Stories of Hope exhibition at the Getty Images Gallery, stating in characteristically blunt fashion of his first meeting with his nephew, 'He was crying, which is just like all babies.' However, when asked what kind of responsibilities he felt he would have as an uncle he added: 'To make sure he has a good upbringing, and to keep him out of harm's way, and make sure he has fun.'

As with the royal wedding two years earlier, the birth of Prince George was the second significant event that served to illustrate how many changes are being made in this very modern royal family. As the future king and queen consort, these changes will affect William and Kate the most, but they will certainly have an impact on Harry also. During the planning of the royal wedding, William's advisors gave him a list of people that they suggested should attend. His heart sank as there read the names of many people he didn't even know. He went to the Queen to seek her counsel and she told him to tear up the list and start again – with his friends at the top of his new list. That piece of advice was one of the first of many changes to protocol within the family.

On the big day, certain traditions were adhered to – the wedding took place in Westminster Abbey, was conducted by the Archbishop of Canterbury, and had the requisite military pomp. However, William and Kate travelled to the ceremony in cars rather than carriages, the wedding breakfast took the form of a buffet featuring miniature sausages and cheese straws rather than a more formal and lavish sit-down meal, and the guest list got smaller and more intimate as the day went on.

Two years later, when Prince George was born William spent the night in hospital with his wife and new son, the first visitors were not royal but the Middletons; and when the new family left the hospital, William strapped the baby-seat into the car and drove his wife and baby back to Kensington Palace himself rather than them all being driven by an aide. Furthermore, rather than spend their first few weeks together in a palace, they spent it in a non-royal residence, and the first picture released to the public of the new family was an amateur shot taken by Kate's father Michael.

Changes are taking place in the roles of royal family members as well. In her early twenties when the Queen was still Princess Elizabeth, she was a full-time working royal, and when Princess Anne left school at eighteen that too was her full-time job. Although Prince Charles went to university and then into a military career, and duty called relatively late at the age of twenty-eight, William was certainly the oldest in his family to enter full-time royal duties at the age of thirty-one. At twenty-nine, Harry is not yet a full-time working member of the royal family as he still has a job in the military, but his family duties have increased significantly over the past year or so. The Queen is now eighty-seven and the Duke of Edinburgh is ninety-two, and although they are still undertaking numerous engagements every year, they are naturally scaling down their workload – now assessing whether or not to undertake overseas travel on a case-by-case basis. Prince Charles is therefore stepping up more to accommodate this. He accompanied the Queen to the official opening of Parliament in May 2013, and later that year he represented his mother at the Commonwealth Heads of

Government meeting in Sri Lanka and at the funeral of Nelson Mandela – both significant occurrences.

Charles's role in state functions over the next few years will continue to increase, and so, naturally, not just William, but Harry too will be called upon to take on more and more royal responsibilities. In the summer of 2013 Prince William left his job as a Search and Rescue pilot and subsequently took on many more engagements. Investitures are the ceremonies – usually held at Buckingham Palace but occasionally at Windsor Castle or the Palace of Holyroodhouse – where knighthoods, CBEs, OBEs and MBEs are bestowed. There are around twenty-five ceremonies a year, and the honours are usually given in person by the Queen, although Prince Charles and Princess Anne sometimes stand in for her. In the summer of 2013, William presided over his first investiture, bestowing among others, an OBE on Andy Murray.

Harry too was embarking on some 'firsts' of his own, which reflect his new, more senior status. He marked national Poppy Day with a visit to the Field of Remembrance at Westminster Abbey with his grandfather the Duke of Edinburgh – the first time the two of them had been on a joint engagement together. He was also proud to be invited to step in for his father on Remembrance Day in the traditional wreath-laying ceremony at the Cenotaph, as Charles and Camilla were on a tour of India. William had been part of the ceremony for four years, but it was the first time Harry had been involved, laying his wreath directly after the Queen and the Duke of Edinburgh but before his brother, as he was representing the Prince of Wales

After seeing in the New Year in Afghanistan and focusing very much on his army career, he had spent the second half of the year supporting his family in this way, as well as strengthening his links to his charity, and therefore cementing a role that he will have for many years to come. He has chosen his affiliations wisely, including those with injured service people; children living with the affects of HIV/AIDS in Africa; and sick children in the UK. These are areas in which he is genuinely interested, and to hear him speak about the causes he supports, there is no doubt that he knows what he is talking about. Not only does he have a full grasp of what has happened in the past, and of the people who are being benefitted by the organizations he's working with, but also he has very strong opinions about the work that needs to be done in the future.

In August 2013, Harry travelled to Angola, where thousands of mines had been planted during the civil war. Years – sometimes decades – later these mines are still to be found there, lying active and lethal but completely concealed. For many Angolan people a chance wrong step could result in death, or a life-changing injury that could damage whole families. The Halo Trust was set up in 1988, aiming to rid not just Angola but numerous other countries of the millions of mines that were still claiming lives and crippling families. Making the land safe means that the people can plant crops, rebuild their homes and raise their children in safety, and in the two-and-a-half decades the organization has been in action, 1.4 million landmines have been destroyed, and 10,423 minefields have been cleared. And while places such as war-torn Mozambique have been completely cleared of mines, in other countries there are estimated to be five more years' work to complete – and in Afghanistan it is estimated that Halo's work will be needed until 2020.

Harry became patron of the Halo Trust's 25th Anniversary Appeal in 2013, and by visiting Angola to see mine clearance projects at work he was very much following in his mother's footsteps. Diana had visited Angola in 1997, and images of her wearing protective equipment walking through minefields are still some of the most enduring images of her. The minefields his mother had visited have all since been safely cleared and are now streets with shops and estate agents, but Harry is only too aware of the amount of work still to be done, and is keen to continue his mother's work. On his visit he focused on Cuito Cuanavale, believed to be one of the heaviest-mined towns in Africa. 'He is irritated about the countries that supplied these landmines are not putting in any funds to clear them twenty-five years later,' revealed Guy Willoughby, the Chief Executive of the Halo Trust. 'He has quite a bee in his bonnet about that, and that is good.'

Harry also attended the WellChild Awards, as he had for the previous four years, as well as a reception for MapAction. He hosted a fund-raising Sentebale dinner in Dubai, and trained with children at Twickenham to promote the Rugby Football Union's All Schools Project in his capacity as patron of the RFU. The All Schools Project aims to encourage all children to be healthy and invested in the team sport. Harry also drew attention to a new facility that brought together two of his areas of interest – the land-mine clearance work of the Halo Trust with the plight of injured service people, when he attended the official opening of the Royal British Legion Centre for Blast Injury Studies, at Imperial College, London. Beneficiaries of the centre will include service people as well as any civilian who has been injured in terrorist attacks or by explosive devices.

He also continued to represent his country. In October 2013 the International Fleet Review was staged in Sydney, Australia, to celebrate the centenary of the first entry of the Royal Australian Navy's Fleet, which had been an event of huge national importance for the country. Harry watched as forty warships from seventeen different nations passed by, and as a million people stood around for over six hours in the sweltering heat to witness the spectacle, the Australian Prime Minister Tony Abbott said, 'I regret to say not every Australian is a monarchist. But today everyone feels like one.' While the Prime Minister's twenty-year-old daughter Bridget posted a picture of her and Harry on Twitter, gushing, 'He's the perfect Prince Charming. I'm single and, well, he's the prince.'

✳

However, Harry's heart was elsewhere. Engagement rumours about him and Cressida Bonas continue to flow, so far with no real substance. Many would like to see Harry 'settled' with a wife, and some crave another royal wedding after the pomp and celebration of the past few years, which have seen in quick succession the engagement of the future king, a full-blown royal wedding, the Diamond Jubilee, and the birth of the new third in line to the throne.

Things do seem to be progressing well for the couple however, and when Harry reached his one-year anniversary with Cressida, she became the only girl he had ever marked that with apart from Chelsy Davy. He and Cressida enjoy normal dating activities – going to James Blunt and Mumford and Sons concerts, dancing to the Rolling Stones at Glastonbury, and watching West End stage show *Book of Mormon*. However, they do seem to be taking it slowly when it comes to progressing their relationship publicly, which was shown when they both attended the Boodles Boxing Ball in September 2013. While Harry's cousins Princesses Beatrice and Eugenie posed with their respective boyfriends Dave Clark and Jack Brooksbank for photographs inside the event, Harry arrived via the front entrance in an explosion of flashbulbs while Cressida arrived with no fanfare through the back entrance. The pair did not pose together for the cameras, nor were they even photographed anywhere near each other.

They have attended two wedding celebrations together – the nuptials of Harry's close childhood friend Thomas van Straubenzee, and the UK-based celebrations for their mutual friend Sam Branson and Cressida's half-sister Isabella Calthorpe. However, Cressida was not present when Harry attended the wedding of his maternal cousin Alexander Fellowes, nor for Prince George's christening, which seemed to be a case of 'no ring, no bring' – spouses of guests were invited but no unmarried partners. However, Harry and Cressida did spend time on the Queen's Sandringham estate together on a weekend break with their friends, and he also took her to his beloved Botswana over the summer.

It seems that the couple are happy as they are for now. As William stated in his engagement interview, the royal family have learned lessons from what has happened in the past, and it seems they now take their time when approaching matters of the heart. The first flush of love is one thing, but the accompanying lifetime of duty, protocol, responsibility and the need for high levels of privacy are quite another. No matter how many changes are taking place, these are things that will always remain, and will need to be accepted by anyone marrying into the royal family. When Princess Anne married Captain Mark Phillips in 1973, they had been together for around fourteen months. When Charles and Diana married in 1981 they had been together for just eleven months, and when Prince Andrew and Sarah Ferguson married in 1986 they had been dating for fifteen months. Each whirlwind marriage sadly ended in divorce. However, Prince Edward and Sophie Rhys-Jones had been together for six years and Peter Phillips and Autumn Kelly had been together five years before they married. The ups and downs of William and Kate's eight-year relationship were well documented, while Harry's cousin Zara and her husband Mike Tindall were also together for eight years before they exchanged vows – and Harry is sure to be paying attention.

Even though Harry has in the past been reckless and headstrong in the heat of the moment and off duty, when it comes to important matters he uses his head – his brother is a good counsel and he also has a good relationship with his father and other senior members of his family. Although Cressida is from an aristocratic background, this only ensures certain things – she is used to mixing in the same circles as Harry, and they also share many of the same interests. But in a bohemian family such as hers, taking on the role of a princess, along with the formality, protocol and restrictions that accompany the role, can be quite a daunting prospect.

*

The lovebirds were separated for a month when Harry embarked on his second trek to raise money for Walking With The Wounded, this time in the Antarctic – and this time it was to be a race, with teams from Great Britain, the USA and the Commonwealth competing to see who reached the South Pole first. Earlier in the year he had flown to Iceland to train, spending time on the Langjökull Glacier with others from his team. This time he would need to complete all of the training as he was to be in the Antarctic for the month-long duration of the trek, rather than the five days he spent on the Arctic expedition in 2011. And this time the conditions would be very different. Those trekking would be at an altitude of 9,000 feet, which because of the spin of the earth is the equivalent of 12–13,000 feet. Not only would they have the wild elements and the gruelling trek itself to contend with, but they would also be feeling the effects of altitude sickness. Additionally, whereas the Arctic had a varied landscape of water pools and ice rubble, the Antarctic is flat and monotonous, which is more mentally challenging.

'You have your iPods to listen to music and mental tricks to get you through it,' explains expedition director Ed Parker. 'We had talked to everyone about the history of the place and imagining those early explorers – Scott, Amundsen, and Shackleton – we said, "Put yourself in their shoes, think about what they were wearing, what they were pulling, the equipment they used to find out where they were in the complete unknown." That makes it far easier when you realize what others went through a hundred years ago.'

It was one of Harry's toughest physical challenges to date, but spurring him on was the thought that the people he was trekking with were going through exactly the same as him, but with serious injuries. His team this time was comprised of Sergeant Duncan Slater, Major Kate Philp, Captain Guy Disney and Captain Ibrar Ali.

Unfortunately, at first, the trek didn't go according to plan. 'After five days we canned the race,' says Parker. 'The guides and the support team were saying it was going to be as flat as a billiards table but because of some bad winter storms, the *sastrugi* (hard ice waves) were far bigger than we were expecting and they went the whole way to the pole.'

The huge amount of extra effort required to move across the

terrain meant that where they were hoping to cover twenty-eight kilometres a day, they were only covering twenty-two or twenty-three. 'That put a lot more stress on the teams right from the beginning,' states Parker. 'Two of the wounded suffered from exhaustion very early on, and three got frostbite. Safety is absolutely paramount and my doctor was getting a little worried.'

It was decided that the three teams would travel together, and Parker explains, 'We were able to move as one and it became a rather more enjoyable and meaningful expedition for everyone. We camped with each other at night rather than in our own individual teams.' The altitude also took its toll on the whole party. Although they all took Diamox, which subdues the effects of altitude sickness, early on some of the participants were medical tent-bound for twenty-four hours as they were treated by the doctor who accompanied the group.

'I'm very glad we had a doctor with us,' recalls Parker. 'Last time the overall party was twelve, and this time it was thirty-two, so the possibility of risk goes up. The most serious incident was with one of the guides who got water on the lung, which comes from altitude. This was his twelfth time to the South Pole and he had never been affected before, so it does show it's very indiscriminate. It took him about three days to get back on his feet.' The entire team of thirty-two suffered from shortness of breath and headaches throughout the trek, including Harry. 'He found the altitude pretty uncomfortable,' states Parker. 'But he's an incredibly strong person actually and he was able to take it in his stride.'

Harry had sustained a broken toe a few weeks before he set off for the Pole, which he admitted to *Sky News* was an 'epic fail', continuing, 'My toe is now ninety-five per cent, so I'm fine. And even if I mention my toe, I see Duncan turn around, laugh at me, mock me, so whatever setback I've had is irrelevant against these guys. It was always going to be.'

Ed Parker adds, 'Harry and I talked about his broken toe in South Africa when we were on our way down, and then I completely forgot about it. It was never in evidence.' Once the initial problems were overcome, the one large team spent the next three weeks making their way to the South Pole, and was sustained by the 'filthy, horrible' food as well as by a different kind of fuel. 'Everyone had a tipple in their sledge,' recalls Parker. 'Whether it was a bottle of vodka or a bottle of whisky, and every now and then a nip of that was very welcome.'

In the evenings the expedition members played cards, read, or listened to audiobooks on their iPads, while Harry took the opportunity to socialize with everyone. 'In the evening he would have supper in different tents,' says Parker. 'I think to break up the scenery but also so he got time with all the different people. Although he was in the UK team it was very noticeable to us all that he was making a conscious effort to spend time with the other two teams as well, which I know was hugely appreciated.'

After a gruelling three-week trek, all teams arrived at the South Pole on 13 December. A bearded and frost-nipped Harry recorded a video message saying what an amazing achievement it was for the injured, adding, 'We've all touched the Pole. We've all had hugs. A few tears here and there.'

That evening they all cooked their own food, as usual, in their tents, before coming together to celebrate. 'That night was a little bit different,' says Parker. 'We were with the whole support team, who had much bigger tents, so we all got together and had a jolly, but it's not like we skied down there with a bar – we maybe had a quarter bottle of whisky here and a half bottle of vodka there. Between thirty people I think we had two bottles that evening.' The expedition members enjoyed even more of a celebration when they got back to the base and devoured their first proper food in almost a month – soup and stew.

*

Harry was back in time to spend a traditional family Christmas at Sandringham. It had been two years since the Queen had all of her family under one roof for the festive season, as the previous year Harry was in Afghanistan and William and Kate were with the Middletons. Much was made in the press of Harry's new beard but Ed Parker explains, 'We all grew beards when we were away. You don't shave while you're there because it's not practical.'

The royal family had a lot to reflect on from the momentous year that had passed, and also to speculate upon in the year to come. In January 2014 it was announced that Harry had completed his attachment to the Army Air Corps and therefore would be stepping down from his job flying Apache helicopters. He was, however, to remain in the military with the rank of Captain in a new desk job. His new role will see him help coordinate 'significant projects and commemorative events involving the army in London', and means that he is now free to try and bring his beloved Warrior Games to the UK.

Harry and William had grown up in Kensington Palace, but for the past ten years their official London residence and later their offices were based in their father's home, Clarence House. However, along with all of the other changes taking place, William, Kate and Harry established their new senior roles by setting up their homes and their office back in Kensington Palace. As William and Kate moved into Apartment 1A in autumn 2013, so Harry also made the move to his permanent new residence of Nottingham Cottage in the palace grounds. He has built a strong team around him. His private secretary was a new addition in 2013, Edward Lane Fox – a former captain in the Blues and Royals and PR for a finance company, and whom Harry has known through his army career, while his personal private secretary is still Helen Asprey. He shares many of his team with William and Kate along with their press secretary Ed Perkins and assistant press secretary Nick Loughran – both of whom moved over from the Buckingham Palace press office. Although Jamie Lowther-Pinkerton left their service full-time in autumn 2013 to work in consultancy, he still works one day a week for them in an advisory capacity. He also remains in their lives as a respected and loved friend, and as such is one of Prince George's godfathers.

As Harry approaches his thirtieth birthday, he is already a man who has done so much. He has helped raise millions of pounds for AIDS orphans in Africa, travelled to the top and the bottom of the world, twice risked his life in the deserts of Afghanistan, lost his heart on more than one occasion, and grown up. It seems the two-year-old boy who launched himself off a table and cut his face open was always going to chase adventure – whether trekking in the Arctic, motorbiking across Africa, or throwing himself into the rigours of military training.

This fearlessness has mostly served Harry well. Especially when tempered with the guidance of his family and, when he was a child, by his nanny Olga Powell and as a young man by Jamie Lowther-Pinkerton. He has been trained to be a lethal weapon if need be, but is also compassionate, intuitive, and playful. The boundary-pushing of his youth that often got him in trouble, has matured into something positive – in evidence when he 'tore up the rulebook' on his first overseas tour, and in his dealings with everyone he meets, from dignitaries, to squaddies, to sick children.

Harry sees himself in three very different roles – soldier, man and prince. However, perhaps it is these clear distinctions that still slip him up from time to time. He feels that when he is operating in an official capacity he is a 'Prince Harry', but the rest of the time he is simply 'Harry' or 'Captain Wales', and should therefore be left alone. The potential problem with this way of thinking is that in fact he is of course all three – constantly. Not one of the roles can be cast off or put on like a piece of clothing depending on the circumstances. Along with William, Kate and Prince George, Harry is the future of the royal family, and although he will have less of an official role to play than his brother, he will be an important support to him while continuing on his own unique path. And from mischievous little boy to high-spirited teenager, and angry young man to wild-hearted warrior prince – no matter what comes next, one thing is for certain: he is sure to keep on surprising.

Picture Credits

Page 1: AP/PA Images (above); Tim Graham/Getty Images (below)

Page 2: Tim Graham/Getty Images (above left); Anwar Hussein/Getty Images (above right); Georges De Keerle (below left); Tim Graham/Getty Images (below right)

Page 3: Tim Graham/Getty Images (all)

Page 4: Rex Features (above); Globe Photos/ImageCollect (below)

Page 5: Duncan Raban/EMPICS/ PA Images (above); David Crump/Daily Mail/Rex Features (below)

Page 6: Antony Jones/UK Press via Getty Images (above); Mike Forster/Daily Mail/Rex Features (below left); Rex Features (below right)

Page 7: Anwar Hussein/EMPICS/PA Images (above); Jayne Fincher/Getty Images (below)

Page 8: Barry Batchelor/PA Images (above); Chip Hires/Gamma-Rapho via Getty Images (below)

Page 9: Rex Features (above); Peter Carrette Archive/Getty Images (below)

Page 10: Rex Features (above); Tim Graham/Getty Images (below)

Page 11: Stephen Hird/AFP/Getty Images (above); Ben Stansall/Getty Images (below)

Page 12: John Stillwell/Anwar Hussein Collection/WireImage/Getty Images (above left); Rex Features (above right); David Cheskin/WPA Pool/Getty Images (below)

Page 13: Rex Features (above); Arthur Edwards/WPA Pool/Getty Images (below)

Page 14: Suzanne Plunkett/Pool/Getty Images (above left); John Stillwell/PA Images (above right); Chris Jackson/Getty Images (below)

Page 15: Nivière/Chamussy/SIPA/Rex Features (above); Coleman-Rayner (below left); David Hartley/Rex Features (below right)

Page 16: John Stillwell/WPA Pool/Getty Images (both)

Bibliography

Wendy Berry, *The Housekeeper's Diary*, Barricade Books, 1995

Gyles Brandreth, *Charles and Camilla*, Century, 2005

Jonathan Dimbleby, *The Prince of Wales: An Intimate Portrait*, Little, Brown, 1994

Chris Hutchins, *Harry*, Robson Press, 2013

Robert Jobson, *Harry's War*, John Blake, 2008

Penny Junor, *Prince William: Born to be King*, Hodder and Stoughton, 2012

Darren McGrady, *Eating Royally*, Rutledge Hill Press, 2007

Andrew Morton, *Diana: Her True Story*, Michael O'Mara, 1998

Katie Nicholl, *William and Harry*, Preface, 2010

Simone Simmons, *Diana: The Last Word*, Orion, 2005

Ken Wharfe, *Diana: Closely Guarded Secret*, Michael O'Mara, 2003

James Wharton, *Out in the Army: My Life as a Gay Soldier*, Biteback Publishing, 2013

Acknowledgements

I very much appreciate everyone who took the time to speak to me for this book, including but not limited to, Ken Wharfe, His Royal Highness Prince Seeiso of Lesotho, Cathy Ferrier, Claire Tomlinson, Ed Parker, John Stillwell, Bryn Parry, Lance Corporal James Wharton (rtd), Captain James A. Kennedy RA (rtd) and Captain Kathryn McGraghan-Hall RAMC (rtd), Justin Adie, Chris Jackson, Liz Hughes, Colin Dyer and Camilla Tominey. I would also like to thank those from the Kensington Palace press office who took the time to speak with me.

Thank you to everyone who has worked hard on this book at my publishers Michael O'Mara, including Louise Dixon who came to me with the idea in the first place, Katy Parker, Judith Palmer, Jessica Barrett, Ana McLaughlin, Ana Bjezancevic, Billy Waqar and Claire Cater. You have all been a complete delight to work with throughout the entire process.

I would also like to say a big thank you for everything to my parents Ralph and Joy Moody, my brother and sister-in-law Stuart and Katherine Moody, and my grandmothers Phyllis Moody and Joan Edwards. Thank you for the feedback and support Catherine Morgan-Smith, Annabel Chapman, Sophie Heal, Annie Tait, David Macdonald, Oliver Grady, Emma Gunavardhana, Paul Green and MDW. An additional thanks goes to the team at Salisbury District Hospital who took such good care of me when I needed surgery for a broken ankle, and was writing this book from my hospital bed ...

Index

INDEX

INDEX

INDEX

INDEX